DK EYEWITNESS

TOP 10
CHICAGO

Top 10 Chicago Highlights

The Top 10 of Everything

CONTENTS

Chicago Area by Area

Streetsmart

Within each Top 10 list in this book, no hierarchy of quality or popularity is implied. All 10 are, in the editor's opinion, of roughly equal merit.

Throughout this book, floors are referred to in accordance with American usage; i.e. the "first floor" is at ground level.

Title page, front cover and spine The Chicago River snaking along skyscrapers downtown
Back cover, clockwise from top left *Interior of the Art Institute of Chicago; Pritzker Pavilion in Millennium Park; McCormick Tribune Ice Rink; Chicago River; Skyline against the lakefront*

The rapid rate at which the world is changing is constantly keeping the DK Eyewitness team on our toes. While we've worked hard to ensure that this edition of Chicago is accurate and up-to-date, we know that opening hours alter, standards shift, prices fluctuate, places close and new ones pop up in their stead. So, if you notice we've got something wrong or left something out, we want to hear about it. Please get in touch at **travelguides@dk.com**

Welcome to
Chicago

Chicago has been called the "City of the Big Shoulders" for its industrial brawn, the "Second City" for its size, and the "Windy City" for its politics – all of which the city embraces with good-humored warmth, and confidence. With DK Eyewitness Top 10 Chicago, it's yours to explore.

The city's own motto is "urbs in horto," or city in a garden, and its connection to nature is readily apparent, from the vast Lake Michigan shoreline to the Chicago River that divides the city – the scenic **Chicago Riverwalk** allows visitors to follow the river as it snakes through the city. Its public living room is the art-filled **Millennium Park**, and its playground is **Navy Pier**, jutting into the lake with carnival-like attractions as well as more high-minded distractions such as the Chicago Shakespeare Theater. The **John G. Shedd Aquarium** offer exposure to natural life beyond the region.

Culture abounds indoors and out. Birthplace of the skyscraper, Chicago has a range of architecture spanning the lofty **Willis Tower** and the earthy Prairie School homes of Frank Lloyd Wright in **Oak Park**. Museums are similarly diverse, from **The Art Institute of Chicago**, stocked with treasures bestowed by civic-minded 19th-century collectors, to the natural history curiosities of the **Field Museum** and the scientific wonders of the **Museum of Science and Industry**. The arts come alive nightly in more than 200 theaters and many jazz and blues clubs in town.

Whether you are visiting for a weekend or longer, our Top 10 guide brings together the best of Chicago, from the hidden neighborhood pubs to **The Magnificent Mile**. The guide has useful tips throughout, from seeking out what's free to getting off the beaten track, plus seven easy-to-follow itineraries tie together a clutch of sights in a short space of time. Add inspiring photography and detailed maps, and you've got the essential pocket-sized travel companion. **Enjoy the book, and enjoy Chicago.**

Clockwise from top: **Chicago skyline, lion statues outside The Art Institute of Chicago,** *Tyrannosaurus rex* **exhibit at the Field Museum, Arthur Heurtley House in Oak Park, The Crystal Gardens at Navy Pier, Jay Pritzker Pavilion in Millennium Park, Botanic Garden**

Exploring Chicago

Thanks to a convenient concentration of attractions, it is easy to cram Chicago's highlights into a few days, or even a weekend. The following two- and four-day itineraries are packed with ideas for you to make the most of your visit, and to fully immerse yourself in the city's sights, sounds, and flavors.

The Magnificent Mile is a great, bustling shopping experience.

Two Days in Chicago

Day ❶
MORNING
Sign up for a **Chicago Architecture Center** cruise *(see p31)* along the Chicago River to get an overview of the city's design prowess. Walk a few blocks south to explore **Millennium Park** *(see pp34–5)*.

AFTERNOON
Take the bridge from the park to **The Art Institute of Chicago** *(see pp14–17)* to admire the Impressionist collection. See the city on high from **Willis Tower** *(see pp12–13)*, enjoy pizza at **Uno's** *(see p61)*, and then catch a comedy show at **Second City** *(see p55)*.

Day ❷
MORNING
Start your day with a visit to the **John G. Shedd Aquarium** *(see pp28–9)* – if you book online in advance, you can skip the line. Afterward, cross the Museum Campus to the famous **Field Museum** *(see pp18–19)*.

AFTERNOON
Make your way to the **Navy Pier** *(see pp24–5)* for a whirl on some of the carnival rides. Then shop at **The Magnificent Mile** *(see pp32–3)*. Finish up at a jazz or blues club *(see pp56–7)*.

Four Days in Chicago

Day ❶
MORNING
Explore the **Chicago Riverwalk** *(see pp30–31)* before taking the **Chicago Architecture Center** cruise *(see p31)*. Disembark at N. Michigan Avenue.

AFTERNOON
Enjoy a hearty lunch at **The Purple Pig** *(see p83)*, then stroll along **The Magnificent Mile** *(see pp32–3)* to take in the city.

Day ❷
MORNING
Browse **The Art Institute of Chicago's** *(see pp14–15)* vast collections. Take the bridge from the Modern Wing into **Millennium Park** *(see pp34–5)*, and lunch at the **Park Grill** *(see pp34–5)*.

Aviation exhibit at the **Museum of Science and Industry**.

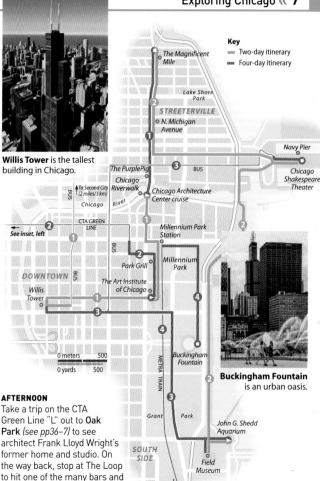

Willis Tower is the tallest
building in Chicago.

Buckingham Fountain
is an urban oasis.

AFTERNOON
Take a trip on the CTA
Green Line "L" out to **Oak
Park** *(see pp36–7)* to see
architect Frank Lloyd Wright's
former home and studio. On
the way back, stop at The Loop
to hit one of the many bars and
restaurants in the area *(see p77)*.

Day ❸
MORNING
Start at the **John G. Shedd Aquarium**
(see pp28–9), then cross the Museum
Campus to marvel at Sue, the giant
Tyrannosaurus rex on display at the
Field Museum *(see pp18–19)*.
AFTERNOON
Admire the city from aloft at the
Willis Tower *(see pp12–13)*. Then
visit **Navy Pier** *(see pp24–5)* for a lake
cruise, dinner, and a performance
at **Chicago Shakespeare Theater**
(see pp25 & 55).

Day ❹
MORNING
Spend the morning exploring the
many exhibits of the **Museum of
Science and Industry** *(see pp20–21)*
at Hyde Park, including the coal
mine and German WWII submarine.
AFTERNOON
Have lunch at the **Valois** cafeteria
(see p105), then take the Metra train
to **Millennium Park** *(see pp34–5)*.
Rent a Divvy bicycle and ride the **Lakefront
Recreational Path** *(see p64)*. After
dark, stroll around the illuminated
Buckingham Fountain *(see p72)*.

Top 10 Chicago Highlights

The modern Jay Pritzker Pavilion in Millennium Park

🔟 Chicago Highlights

The Midwest's largest city, Chicago is a perfect blend of big-city sophistication and small-town hospitality. Impressive architecture, cuisines for all budgets and tastes, great shopping experiences, diverse neighborhoods, outstanding museums, and a lakefront setting make this city a must-visit place.

① Willis Tower and Its Views

The city's tallest skyscraper is actually made up of nine tube-like sections. The views are awesome: on a clear day, you can see up to 50 miles (81 km) from the 103rd-floor Skydeck (see pp12–13).

② The Art Institute of Chicago

This grande dame of Chicago's art scene features world-renowned collections. The Impressionist section is outstanding (see pp14–17).

③ Field Museum

Delve into cultures and environments from ancient Egypt to modern Africa, via Midwestern wildlife, and the underground life of bugs. The Field also offers a closeup of the world's most complete *Tyrannosaurus rex* skeleton (see pp18–19).

④ Museum of Science and Industry

This museum is the only building left from the 1893 World's Columbian Exposition. Interactive exhibits range from space exploration to coal mining, including a ride on the Silver Streak train (see pp20–21).

5 Navy Pier
Once a tourist trap, this Lake Michigan pier is now a bustling year-round playground. In warm weather, take a boat tour or join the throngs that stroll along the pier and get some amazing city views (see pp24–5).

John G. Shedd Aquarium 6
Chicago's aquarium on the lakefront houses thousands of marine animals, from big beluga whales to tiny seahorses. Get a fish-eye view at the Oceanarium's underwater viewing galleries (see pp28–9).

7 Chicago Riverwalk
Snaking along the Chicago River, this mile-long promenade is lined with attractions including outdoor art installations, museums, restaurants, and boat- and kayak-rental services (see pp30–31).

8 The Magnificent Mile
Chicago's top shopping destination is a four-lane stretch of North Michigan Avenue. It is also home to a few buildings that survived the Great Chicago Fire of 1871 (see pp32–3).

9 Millennium Park
Opened in 2004, Millennium Park has many attractions that are a magnet for locals and visitors alike (see pp34–5).

10 Frank Lloyd Wright's Oak Park
Frank Lloyd Wright, the creator of Prairie Style architecture, was based in this Chicago suburb for 20 years. His legacy is an "outdoor museum" of 25 buildings. Take a self-guided or guided tour of his creations (see pp36–7).

Greater Chicago

NORTHSIDE

Oak Park 10

NORTH AVE
CENTRAL AVE
WESTERN AVENUE

EISENHOWER EXPRESSWAY

CICERO

area of map left

STEVENSON EXPRESSWAY

DAN RYAN EXPWY

FAR SOUTH 4

0 km 5
0 miles 5

River WACKER DRIVE

STREET
STREET
STREET
AVENUE

NORTH LAKE SHORE DRIVE

Navy Pier Park

Gateway Park

5

RANDOLPH STREET

Monroe Harbor

Lake Michigan

SOUTH LAKE SHORE DRIVE

Museum Campus 6
3

★ Willis Tower and Its Views

It might have lost the US's tallest building slot, but Willis Tower is still the second tallest in the country, at 1,450 ft (442 m), and home to the nation's highest observation deck. The tower uses nine exterior frame tubes, avoiding the need for interior supports. For 360-degree views of the city, head to the 103rd-floor Skydeck, where the brave can also step into a series of glass boxes that provide fascinating views straight down to the ground.

1 John Hancock Center

The Willis Tower's North Side counterpart (see p79) is this 100-story skyscraper. It houses a retail area, offices, and apartments – as well as an open-air observatory.

2 Soldier Field

Home to the Chicago Bears football team (see p67) for over 30 years, the lakeside stadium (above), which opened in 1924, saw the addition of a 67,000-seat structure in 2003.

3 Marina City

When built in 1964, these 60-story buildings (left), nicknamed the corncobs (see p42), were once the tallest residential structures in the world.

NEED TO KNOW

MAP J4 ■ 233 S. Wacker Dr. (entrance on Jackson Blvd.) ■ "L" Station: Quincy/Wells (Orange, Purple, Brown & Pink lines) ■ 312-875-9696 ■ www.theskydeck.com

Open Mar–Sep: 9am–10pm daily; Oct–Feb: 10am–8pm daily

Adm Skydeck: $35; children (3–11): $26

Soldier Field: 425 E. McFetridge Dr.

Marina City: 300 N. State St.

United Center: 1901 W. Madison St.

McCormick Place: 2301 S. Lake Shore Dr.

- - - - - - - - - - - -

■ The tower has eight restaurants to pick from.

■ Opt for an audio Sky Tour at the Skydeck's 16 viewing points.

■ Check visibility levels at the security desk before heading to the Skydeck.

④ Chicago River

The 156-mile-(250-km-) long Chicago River tops world records with its 43 opening bridges. In 1900, an amazing engineering feat resulted in the reversal of the river flow (see p40). Every St. Patrick's Day the main branch is dyed green.

⑦ Lake Michigan

This is the third largest of the five Great Lakes. Water temperatures struggle to hit tepid during summer, but many beach-goers swim nevertheless. On a clear day, you can often see across to the shores of Indiana and Michigan.

TOP 10 TOWER FACTS

1 It is 110 stories high
2 It weighs a massive 222,500 tons
3 The tower took three years to construct
4 Building costs topped $150 million
5 It contains over 2,000 miles (3,220 km) of electric cables …
6 … And 25,000 miles (40,233 km) of piping
7 25,000 people enter and exit each day
8 1.7 million visit the Skydeck each year
9 The elevators travel at an ear-popping 1,600 ft (490 m) per minute
10 Six automatic machines wash its 16,100 windows

Willis Tower dominating the Chicago skyline

⑤ United Center

This vast indoor sports arena and concert venue is also known as "the house that Michael built," as it was basketball player Michael Jordan's fame that attracted the money to fund it. Outside, there's a statue of him.

⑧ Merchandise Mart

One of the world's largest commercial buildings (in floor area) (see p79), this 1930s structure was run by the Kennedy family until the late 1990s.

⑨ McCormick Place

The first convention center opened here in 1960 but burned down. Architect Helmut Jahn built the second in 1971 at twice the size with 40,000 sprinkler heads. It attracts nearly 3 million visitors a year. Four buildings now make up this complex, and are connected by a shop-lined promenade.

⑩ Navy Pier

A former naval base turned fun-filled mecca (see pp24–5), and Chicago's top attraction.

Grant Park ⑥

Built entirely on a landfill following the Great Chicago Fire (see p40), this pretty park **(right)** is one of the city's largest and is the site of the summer music festivals (see p48).

TOP 10 ★ The Art Institute of Chicago

Guarded by iconic lions and up a flight of grand stone steps, is the Midwest's largest art museum. Housed in a massive Beaux-Arts edifice with an impressive Modern Wing by Renzo Piano, the Institute has thousands of works from around the globe, and is famous for its Impressionist and Post-Impressionist collections.

4 Nighthawks
One of the most famous images in 20th-century American art, this 1942 painting **(left)** by Realist Edward Hopper has a melancholy quality. It includes a depiction of fluorescent lighting, new at the time to US cities.

1 Acrobats at the Cirque Fernando
Children were often the subjects of Renoir's sunny paintings: this luminous 1879 work shows a circus owner's daughters taking a bow after their act.

3 The Old Guitarist
A young, struggling Picasso painted this tortured 1903 portrait during his Blue Period. It reflected his grief over a friend's suicide and was a precursor to his own style of Cubism.

2 American Gothic
Grant Wood borrowed from the detailed style of the Flemish Renaissance art to create this painting (1930). Though perceived by many as satirical, the painting **(right)** celebrates the traditions and culture of the midwest.

5 Stacks of Wheat Series
From 1890 to 1891, Monet painted 30 views of the haystacks that stood outside his house in France. This museum has six, which illustrate the Impressionist doctrine of capturing the fleeting effects of light in nature.

NEED TO KNOW

MAP L4 ■ 111 S. Michigan Ave ■ "L" Station: Adams (Green, Orange, Purple, Brown & Pink lines), Monroe (Blue & Red lines) ■ 312-443-3600 ■ www.artic.edu

Open 11am–6pm Sat–Mon, 11am–9pm Thu–Fri

Adm adults $25; students, seniors and children 14 yrs and older $19; under-14s free

■ Terzo Piano located in the Modern Wing is perfect for a fine-dining lunch with city views. Alternatively, you can cross over to GePaDe Caffe (60 E. Adams St.) for some great panini.

■ The institute allows visitors to join a free, hour-long introductory tour. Meet in gallery 100 (noon daily, and 2pm Tue, Wed, and Fri).

■ Don't miss the reconstruction of the 1893 Stock Exchange Trading Room.

Museum Guide
The Art Institute is the second-largest art museum in the US. Locations of works and accessibility of specific galleries are subject to change. If there's a particular work that you want to see, check in advance to ensure it is on view.

6 At the Moulin Rouge

Unlike many of his fellow Impressionists who painted serene scenes, Toulouse-Lautrec was drawn to the exuberant nightlife of Paris. This dramatic painting (1892) celebrates the Moulin Rouge cabaret **(above)**.

8 America Windows

Unveiled at the Art Institute in 1977, Marc Chagall's stunning stained-glass windows were a gift to the city he loved. The six vibrant panels depict the US as a place of cultural and religious freedom.

10 The Herring Net

Winslow Homer honed his Realist skills as an illustrator for magazines. After moving to Maine, he created a series of images, including this one (1885), depicting man's complex relationship with the sea.

7 A Sunday on La Grande Jatte – 1884

Massive and mesmerizing, this painting took Georges Seurat two years to complete. The scene is created from dots of color, based on his study of optical theory, later known as pointillism.

9 The Child's Bath

The only American to exhibit in Paris with the Impressionists, Mary Cassatt often portrayed women and children as in this **(left)**, her most famous painting (1893). Her domestic subjects reflect the limited freedom of women at the time.

Key to Floorplan
- Lower level
- First level
- Second level
- Third level

Museum Floorplan

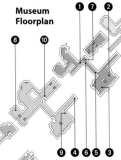

🔟 Collections

Two Sisters, by Pierre August Renoir, a highlight of the European Collection

1 European Collection

Arranged chronologically, and spanning the Middle Ages through 1950, this prodigious collection includes a significant array of Renaissance and Baroque art and sculpture. However, its main draw is a body of nearly 400 Impressionist and Post-Impressionist paintings. Instrumental in its creation was Bertha Honoré Palmer who acquired over 40 Impressionist works (largely ignored in France at the time) for the 1893 World's Columbian Exposition.

Arthur Rubloff paperweight

2 American Arts

This impressive holding contains some 5,500 paintings and sculptures dating from the 1600s to 1950. In addition, paintings and works on paper are on loan from the Terra Foundation collection, and there is a range of decorative arts, including furniture, glass, and ceramics from the 18th century through to the present. The silver collection is especially noteworthy.

3 Arthur Rubloff Collection of Paperweights

This fabulous assemblage numbers in excess of 1,400 paperweights, making it one of the largest of its kind in the world. It displays colorful and exquisite examples from all periods, designs, and techniques. The paperweights mostly originate from 19th-century France, though some were made in America and the United Kingdom. Displays also reveal the secrets of how paperweights are made.

4 Arms and Armor

The Harding Collection of Arms and Armor is one of the largest in America. On permanent display are over 200 items related to the art of war, including weapons, and complete and partial suits of armor for soldiers – as well

Arms and armor exhibits

as horses. The items displayed originate from Europe, the US, and the Middle East, and date from the 15th through the 19th centuries.

5 Architecture

Given the city's strong architectural heritage and focus, it is not surprising that Chicago's Art Institute boasts an architecture and design department, one of only a few in the US. Sketches and drawings are accessible by appointment, and changing public displays feature models, drawings, and architectural pieces, such as a stained-glass window by Frank Lloyd Wright.

6 Modern and Contemporary Art

This important collection represents the significant art movements in Europe and the US from 1950 to the present day, including a strong body of Surrealist works, and paintings by Picasso, Matisse, and Kandinsky, as well as showing how American artists, such as Georgia O'Keeffe, interpreted European Modernism.

7 Thorne Miniature Rooms

Narcissa Ward Thorne, a Chicago art patron, combined her love of miniatures with her interest in interiors and decorative arts to create the 68 rooms in this unique Lilliputian installation. Some of the 1 inch:1 foot scale rooms are replicas of specific historic interiors, while others are period recreations,

One of Thorne's miniature rooms

combining features copied from various sites or based on illustrations and other records of period furniture.

8 Photography

Spanning the history of the medium, from its origins in 1839 to the present, this eminent collection was started by Georgia O'Keeffe in 1949 with the donation of works by Alfred Stieglitz. Many modern masters, including Julien Levy, Edward Weston, Paul Strand, and Eugène Atget, are represented.

9 Asian Art

This sizeable collection covers 5,000 years and features Japanese screens, Chinese ceramics and jades, and Southeast Asian sculpture. The museum's assemblage of Japanese woodblock prints, such as *Courtesan* (c.1705–1715) by Kaigetsudo Dohan, is one of the most impressive outside Japan. Look out, too, for the rare early 14th-century scroll painting, *Legends of the Yuzu Nembutsu Sect*.

10 The Arts of Africa

Completely reinstalled in 2019, this gallery displays artifacts, sculptures, furniture, masks, jewelry, beadwork, and metalwork from all across the continent. Exhibits are divided into four overarching regions: Northern Africa and the Sahel, Coastal West Africa, Central Africa, and Eastern and Southern Africa. A fifth section focuses exclusively on ceramics and textiles. Accompanying this newly refreshed gallery are digital labels and a new audio tour.

Museum Floorplan

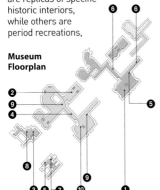

🔟 ⭐ Field Museum

Founded in 1893 to display items from the World's Columbian Exposition, and renamed in 1905 to honor its first major benefactor, Marshall Field, this vast museum offers fascinating insights into global cultures and environments past and present. Home to all sorts of cultural treasures, fossils, and artifacts, as well as to myriad interactive exhibits, make no bones about it: this natural history museum is one of the best in the country.

Sue ①
A *Tyrannosaurus rex* (**right**), 13-ft (4-m) high by 42-ft (12.8-m) long – one of the largest and best preserved ever found – is on display here. Its real 600-lb (272-kg) skull is on view nearby.

② Crown Family PlayLab
Six themed areas, from a scientist's lab to a dinosaur dig, are full of things for kids to discover.

③ Grainger Hall of Gems
Fiber-optic lighting magically illuminates over 500 glittering gems, precious stones, and minerals. Even though it's a replica, the star of the show is the breathtaking Hope Diamond (**left**).

NEED TO KNOW

MAP L6 ■ 1400 S. Lake Shore Dr. ■ Metra station: Roosevelt Rd.
■ 312-922-9410
■ www.fieldmuseum.org

Open 9am–5pm daily

Adm: adults $340, children (3–11) $29, seniors and students with ID $35

■ Grab a bite under the watchful gaze of dinosaur Sue at the Corner Bakery (main level).

■ Two free trolley services link the Field, the Shedd (*see pp28–9*), and the Art Institute (*see pp16–17*) with the nearest Metra and CTA stations as well as with downtown.

■ Have a museum-related question? Look out for attendants carrying a big "Ask Me" sign.

Museum Guide
The main entrance is located on the museum's north side, though visitors typically enter on the south, where buses, trolleys, and cabs drop off. A third (first level) west entrance is suitable for wheelchair access. If you visit on a weekday, it's worth asking staff about the museum's Free Highlights Tours, which take place twice daily. Don't forget to look for information on the day's special events, tours, and activities, posted throughout the building.

4 Inside Ancient Egypt

This part-original, part-replica Egyptian ruin leads you up and down stairs, into Egyptian bedrooms and tombs, and through a marketplace. See how Cleopatra lived and how mummies were wrapped.

7 Africa

Browse the wares of a Saharan market, experience life on a slave ship, and see a pair of fighting elephants: this exhibit **(right)** offers an amazing and educational journey through ancient and modern Africa for all ages.

8 Pacific Spirits

A celebration of vibrant Pacific islander culture: visitors can see dramatic masks, listen to recorded sounds from the swamps of New Guinea, and bang on an impressive 9-ft (3-m) drum.

9 Evolving Planet

Journey through four billion years of life on Earth as a wide range of displays tell the story of evolution. Interact with single-celled organisms, giant dinosaurs, and our first human ancestors.

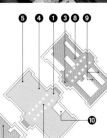

Museum Floorplan

Key to Floorplan

- First level
- Main level
- Upper level

5 Lions of Tsavo

In 1898, these two partners in crime killed and ate 140 men who were constructing a bridge in Kenya, before they in turn were hunted and killed. The skins were first used as rugs, before being mounted as you see today.

10 The Ancient Americas

Step into the world of Ice Age mammoth-hunters, enter an 800-year-old pueblo, and explore the Aztec Empire, as artifacts **(left)** and displays uncover 13,000 years of human history in the Americas.

6 Underground Adventure

Enter this larger-than-life "subterranean" ecosystem to get a bug's-eye view of life. Wander through a jungle of roots **(right)**, and listen to the chatter of a busy ant colony. Extra admission charged.

⭐ Museum of Science and Industry

The cultural star of the city's South Side, this museum was the first in North America to introduce interactive exhibits, with a record of innovative, hands-on displays dating back to the 1930s. More than one million visitors flock annually to this vast Neo-Classical building, which houses more than 800 exhibits and is a Chicago must-see, especially for families. Make sure you arrive rested, since it takes a whole day to hit just the top attractions.

1 Henry Crown Space Center
This, the first manned spacecraft to orbit the moon, offers a peek into the 1960s space race. Historic photos, space suits, and a training module set the scene.

3 Coal Mine
Venture down a simulated 600 ft (184 m) in an authentic shaft elevator to discover how coal was extracted in the 1930s compared to today. The mini train ride enhances the underground illusion.

4 Giant Dome Theater
The films shown in this five-story theater make the viewers feel like they are right in the thick of the on-screen action and adventures. On a rotating program, the films are screened approximately every 50 minutes.

2 Science Storms
This two-story exhibit **(above)** illustrates basic principles of physics and chemistry using recreations of natural phenomena, including a 40-ft (12-m) tornado, a giant Tesla coil that produces lighting, and a 30-ft (9-m) wave tank.

5 YOU! The Experience
Discover aspects of the human body and mind from a new perspective. The centerpiece of this exhibit is the giant 13-ft- (4-m-) tall animated 3-D human heart, which offers a fascinating interactive experience.

7 ToyMaker 3000
Twelve robotic arms work the assembly line to produce toy top after colorful top in this display of computer integrated manufacturing technology. Race a robot to see who can trace letters faster. Souvenir tops are $5.

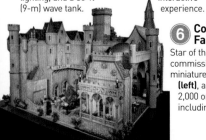

6 Colleen Moore's Fairy Castle
Star of the silent screen, Colleen Moore commissioned the design of this lavish miniature castle, a study in craftsmanship **(left)**, and lovingly filled it with over 2,000 one-twelfth-scaled objects, including the world's smallest Bible.

Museum Floorplan

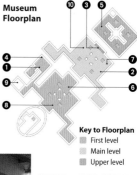

Key to Floorplan
First level
Main level
Upper level

8 All Aboard the Silver Streak
Both Art Deco design aficionados and rail buffs are drawn to this stream-lined, vintage Zephyr train **(above)** with its ground-breaking diesel-electric engine.

10 The Great Train Story
Over 20 miniature trains race past skyscrapers, through prairies, and over the Rockies to the Pacific Docks on 1,425 ft (437 m) of track **(above)** that replicate the 2,200-mile (3,540-km) train trip from Chicago to Seattle on this interactive model railroad.

9 U-505 Submarine
Take a tour around this original 1941 German U-boat **(above)**. The submarine was captured during World War II and still looks much like it did then, complete with an Enigma code-breaking machine.

NEED TO KNOW

MAP F6 ▪ 57th Sts & Lake Shore Dr. ▪ Metra station: 55th /56th/57th Sts.
▪ 1-773-684-1414
▪ www.msichicago.org

Open 9:30am–5:30pm Tue–Sun; Adm: adults $22, children (3–11) $13

▪ Options for food are plentiful: try the Museum Park Café or Finnigan's Sandwich Shoppe, which offer snacks and drinks.

▪ Advance tickets can be reserved on the Internet or via telephone. They may cost extra, but are worth it on busy weekends.

▪ Additional special experience tickets are sold at all museum entrances. Prices vary.

Museum Guide
The museum has two main entrances – the Great Hall (first level) and the Henry Crown Space Center (for the Omnimax Theater). Visit the tour-only displays (Silver Streak, U-505, the Coal Mine) before heading to the Omnimax as there can be more than an hour's wait later on. Strollers can be rented in the Great Hall.

🔟 Exhibits

Transportation Gallery

6 The Art of the Bicycle
This fascinating exhibit explores the pioneering evolution of the bicycle over the last 200 years.

7 Ships Through the Ages
Here, model ships chart marine transportation from Egyptian sailboats through to modern ocean liners. Highlights include scale versions of Christopher Columbus's three ships.

1 Transportation Gallery
A full-size Boeing 727 and a British World War II fighter plane dangle dramatically above a steam locomotive and the world's fastest land vehicle, while visitors explore the forces of flight via engaging computer games and videos.

2 U-505
Artifacts, archival footage, and interactive challenges bring to life this restored U-505 German submarine. Optional on-board tours of the boat are available.

3 Genetics and the Baby Chick Hatchery
Explore the complex and controversial world of genetics and genetic engineering and learn how cloning is possible.

4 Farm Tech
Learn about life on today's farms and the modern technologies that get food from the field to your table. Children can ride in a real combine and take part in a cow-milking challenge.

5 Numbers in Nature: A Mirror Maze
The world of cyberspace comes alive here via educational yet fun hands-on displays.

8 The Swiss Jolly Ball
The world's largest pinball machine has been here since 1998. Watch the pinball race through Swiss-themed scenery and admire its complicated mechanics.

9 The Whispering Gallery
This exhibit has been at the museum since 1938, and still delights passers by. It shows through design how sound waves travel to make the faintest whisper audible at the other end of a room.

10 Slime Science
One of the museum's popular Live Science Experiences, this exhibit provides insight into the science of using everyday household items to make sticky-icky slime.

Museum Floorplan

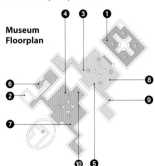

THE MUSEUM'S ORIGINS

Built as the Palace of Fine Arts in 1893, the Museum of Science and Industry is the only building left from Daniel Burnham's "White City." This was built for the World's Columbian Exposition, marking the 400th anniversary (albeit one year late) of Christopher Columbus's arrival in the New World. Burnham, the Director of Works for the fair *(see p43)*,

Ferris Wheel

commissioned architects like Charles Atwood to create structures that would showcase the best in design, culture, and technology. The Field Museum *(see pp18–19)* inhabited the building until the 1920s when it moved to its Museum Campus home. Sears Roebuck retail chief Julius Rosenwald then decided that a fortified palace, stripped to its steel frame and rebuilt in limestone, would be the perfect home for a new museum devoted to "industrial enlightenment" and US technological triumphs. The Museum launched around 1933 when Chicago hosted its next World's Fair, Century of Progress Exposition.

**TOP 10
FEATURES OF THE
1893 EXPOSITION**

1 First ever Ferris Wheel

2 Palace of Fine Arts

3 Midway Plaisance, first separate amusement area at a world's fair

4 Jackson Park, landscaped by designer Frederick Law Olmsted

5 The "Streets of Cairo" exhibit

6 The nickname "Windy City" was introduced *(see p113)*

7 A 1,500 lb (680 kg) chocolate Venus de Milo

8 A 70-ft- (21-m-) high tower of light bulbs

9 Floodlights used on buildings for the first time

10 250,000 separate displays on show

The Museum of Science and Industry building started out as the Palace of Fine Arts in 1893.

Present-day Museum of Science and Industry building

TOP10 ★ Navy Pier

Back in 1995, Chicago's Navy Pier was a drab slab of concrete projecting into Lake Michigan, formerly used as a military and freight terminal. But a huge effort to attract locals and tourists resulted in the installation of a variety of attractions on the waterfront – for kids as well as adults – that draw over nine million people annually, making this Chicago's most visited attraction. The Pier underwent extensive renovations for its 100th anniversary in 2016.

4 Musical Carousel

A quaint merry-go-round of 36 hand-painted horses and chariots next to the Ferris Wheel replicates a similar ride installed on the Pier in the 1920s.

5 Centennial Wheel

It's hard to miss the Pier's 196-ft- (60-m-) high ferris wheel **(right)**, installed in 2016 to replace its smaller predecessor. The ride seats eight in each of its 42 enclosed cars. Daytime rides offer fine lake views, while at night, light shows projected onto the wheel create colorful displays.

1 Wave Swinger

Each of the 48 chain-suspended chairs on this old-fashioned thrill ride **(above)** lifts riders 14 ft (5 m) in the air, and spins them until the skyline blurs.

2 IMAX® Theatre

The six-story movie theater offers celluloid fare ranging from scientific documentaries to Disney features. Sound and vision headsets aid 3-D movie fun.

3 Polk Bros Park

Navy Pier's front yard features a dramatic fountain with around 250 programmable jets that mimic the movement of water, schools of fish, or flocks of birds. In winter, the park converts into an ice rink.

6 New Food Experience

Replacing run-of-the-mill boardwalk fare, the Pier's newly revamped food court includes several satellites of Chicago-based restaurants such as the two North Side favorites, DMK Burger Bar and Fish Bar.

7 Chicago Children's Museum

Kids love this hands-on museum **(below)** that educates through play. Under-twos get dedicated spaces, including a water room *(see p52)*.

Navy Pier Plan

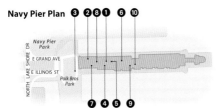

NEED TO KNOW

MAP M3 ■ 600 E. Grand Ave. ■ CTA Bus: 29, 65, 56, 66, 120, 121 ■ 1-800-595-7437 ■ www.navypier.com

Open summer: 10am–10pm daily (to midnight Fri & Sat); Sep & Oct: 10am–8pm Mon–Sat (to 10pm Fri & Sat); winter: 10am–8pm Mon–Sat (to 10pm Fri & Sat), 10am–7pm Sun

Adm: Free, but many attractions charge

■ Skip the chain eateries for ribs and live jazz at Joe's Be-Bop Café.

■ In summer the beer garden at the far end of the Pier has stellar city views and free bands.

■ Join a 90-minute lake tour *(see p114)* on a four-masted schooner, or take a ride on a Seadog speedboat.

■ Save money and time spent waiting in line by purchasing a combination ticket for the Musical Carousel, Centennial Wheel, and Wave Swinger.

Orientation
Take public transit, a taxi, or walk to Navy Pier. If driving, you'll find over 1,600 parking spaces right on the Pier. Once there, be sure to stop off at the Guest Services desk, just inside the main entrance, to pick up a schedule for details of the day's events, including performance times and locations for the resident comedy troupe, brass band, and an acapella singing group.

9 Chicago Shakespeare Theater

This highly respected theater aims to make the Bard accessible to the pleasure-seeking masses visiting Navy Pier. As well as the Shakespearean standards performed here, productions also include the "Short Shakespeare" series for younger audiences.

10 Amazing Chicago's Funhouse Maze

This mirror-filled, Chicago-themed walking maze leads you on a disorienting, 15-minute journey. Expect spinning lights, startling sound effects, and new perspectives on the city's history and sights. It is an ideal rainy-day attraction.

Crystal Gardens 8

One of the most beautiful sights on the Navy Pier is the Crystal Gardens, a miniature botanical oasis located within a glass-domed atrium **(right)**. Filled with 80 towering palm trees, twinkling fairy lights, and fountains, it is a particularly magical spot on winter days and is frequently used as a special events venue for weddings and parties.

Following pages Aerial view across the city to Lake Michigan

TOP 10 ★ John G. Shedd Aquarium

The eponymous John G. Shedd, president of Marshall Field's department store, donated this Beaux-Arts aquarium to Chicago in 1929. One of the city's top attractions, it houses some 32,000 marine animals representing 1,500 different species that include amphibians, fish, and aquatic mammals. The latter can be seen in the saltwater of the glass-walled Oceanarium, which places an infinity pool in front of Lake Michigan to transporting effect.

1 Caribbean Reef

This vibrant tropical tank **(left)** contains glinting tarpon, bonnethead sharks, fluttering rays, and many other fish. A scuba diver hand-feeds them several times daily, narrating his task via an underwater microphone.

2 Polar Play Zone

Set in Shedd's basement, this play zone lets you explore the Arctic waters in a submarine with interactive features. Visitors can try on penguin suits in the Icy South play area. There is an underwater viewing area too.

3 Virtual Reality

As well as in-person animal encounters, Shedd offers immersive VR experiences. These live-action journeys allow participants, wearing VR goggles, to swim with humpback whales off the Islands of Tonga.

4 Waters of the World

Themed exhibits hold more than 90 re-created aquatic habitats, including Tropical Waters, Ocean Coasts, and the rivers, lakes, and lagoons of Australia, Africa, Asia, and even Chicago's local water bodies.

5 Wild Reef

Gain a daring diver's perspective of whitetip reef, blacktip reef, sand-bar, and zebra sharks **(above)**. The sawfish and fearsome lionfish happily hold their own amid the predator school.

Exterior view of the Shedd

NEED TO KNOW

MAP M6 ▪ 1200 S. Lake Shore Dr. ▪ "L" station: Roosevelt (Green, Orange, & Red lines) ▪ 312-939-2438 ▪ www.shedd aquarium.org

Open 9am–6pm daily

Adm adults $39.95; children (3–11) & seniors $29.95; aquatic show an additional $2

▪ Choose from two dining options at the Shedd.

Soundings serves a full line of Starbucks drinks and coffee, fresh-baked pastries, and sandwiches. The Bubble Net Food Court features iconic local foods such as the Chicago dog, pizza, sustainable-sourced fish and chips, house-made soups, and artisan grain bowls.

▪ Don't miss the underwater viewing galleries.

▪ Check out Jazzin' at the Shedd on Wednesdays

(5–10pm, adm $39.99 adults, $29.99 children 3–11) from June to August.

Aquarium Guide
Consult the day's event schedule printed on the map you're given. Be sure to arrive 10–15 minutes early for an Oceanarium Show to get the best seats, and remember that the 20–30-minute Habitat Chats often follow on after the shows.

⑥ Special Exhibit Gallery

This quaint 3,600-sq-ft (334-sq-m) special exhibit gallery is on the mezzanine level of the Oceanarium and features changing exhibits focused on aquatic animals.

⑦ 4-D Experience

This hi-tech theater experience has "special FX seats" that bombard spectators with bubbles, wind, smells, sounds, and other surprises.

⑧ Amazon Rising

Demonstrating the huge seasonal tides of the world's second longest river, this exhibit presents a year in the Amazon flood plain.

⑨ Habitat Chats

Observe sharks close up and learn how they interact with the whole reef community, discover the evolutionary adaptations of sea lions, beluga whales, and dolphins, and investigate the features of penguins.

⑩ Abbott Oceanarium

Underwater galleries **(left)** afford incredible views of the likes of dolphins and beluga whales swimming through the Oceanarium's vast pools. It is bordered by rocky outcrops and towering pines in a re-creation of the Pacific Northwest coast.

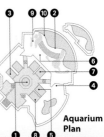

Aquarium Plan

TOP 10 ⭐ Chicago Riverwalk

Complementing the gently winding Chicago River for a generous 1.25-mile (2-km) stretch is the modern Chicago Riverwalk, opened in 2016. Treating pedestrians to fabulous art, architecture, and recreation, the Riverwalk serves almost as a microcosm of the entire city. During the warmer months, the area buzzes with patrons enjoying al fresco dining and picnics with a view of kayakers and boat tours; in colder months, pedestrians bundle up for scenic waterside strolls.

3 Public Art
From intricate tile mosaics to larger-than-life cast-aluminum flowers, public art of all shapes and sizes adds color and texture to the arcades and plazas along the Riverwalk.

4 Playground
Down on the east end of the Riverwalk is a kids' entertainment zone with Playworld's award-winning PlayCubes®, as well as brightly colored sculptures situated on rubber flooring.

1 River Theater
The main "performance" here is the Chicago River itself. Stretching from Upper Wacker drive all the way down to the water, the open-air auditorium-like seating **(above)** offers visitors views of the river, with trees integrated for shady spots.

2 Art on theMART
After dark, make your way to the Riverwalk's western end to catch the latest edition of Art on theMART: dazzling public art installations projected onto the Merchandise Mart building. Featuring works by contemporary artists, projections are displayed nightly at 9pm and 9:30pm.

5 McCormick Bridgehouse & Chicago River Museum
The landmark five-story McCormick Bridgehouse is home to an interesting museum tracing the city's relationship with the river and offering insights into the mechanical magic of Chicago's bridgehouses. It is open for ticketed tours and hosts exhibitions as well as free lunchtime lectures.

6 Vietnam Veterans Memorial Plaza
In a quiet corner, a set of grassy ledges and a rectangular fountain pay homage to the Vietnam War. A stone wall **(below)** is inscribed with the names of those who died.

7 Chicago Water Taxi

Though it's technically a commuter boat, the Chicago Water Taxi doubles as a cheap and easy "cruise" along the Chicago River. It makes stops at Michigan Avenue, Chinatown, and Ogilvie/Union Station, across from the Willis Tower.

Chicago Riverwalk Map

The glittering Chicago Riverwalk

8 Dining Options

From full-service dining at City Winery **(below)** to the beer garden at The Northman to satellite mom-and-pop cafés, there are quite a few options for dining along the water's edge.

9 CAC and Chicago's First Lady Cruises

A fantastic way to take in the city's skyline is the architecture cruise aboard Chicago's First Lady vessel. It is run by the Chicago Architecture Center (CAC), which also organizes walking, train, and boat tours (see p111).

10 Floating Gardens

At the Jetty is a series of floating wetlands and water gardens. Part of a larger ecological installation, they are intended to help grow and maintain the river's natural wildlife habitat.

NEED TO KNOW

MAP M3 ■ "L" Station: Clark/Lake, State/Lake (Blue, Brown, Green, Orange, Pink & Purple lines) ■ www.chicago riverwalk.us

Art on theMART: 222 W. Merchandise Mart Plaza; www.artonthemart.com

Playground: 590 E. Wacker Dr.

McCormick Bridgehouse & Chicago River Museum: 99 Chicago Riverwalk; www.bridgehouse museum.org

Vietnam Veterans Memorial Plaza: 330 Chicago Riverwalk

Chicago Water Taxi: www. chicagowatertaxi.com

CAC and Chicago's First Lady Cruises: 112 E. Wacker Dr.; www. architecture.org

■ Experienced kayakers can opt for hourly rentals from Urban Kayaks (*425 E. Riverwalk S.*).

TOP 10 ★ The Magnificent Mile

This glitzy strip of stores and striking buildings runs for, you guessed it, about a mile (1.6 km), along North Michigan Avenue. A sharp developer came up with the "magnificent" moniker in 1947, and it has stuck ever since. Often known as The Mag Mile, it is home to department stores like Neiman Marcus, as well as high-end boutiques such as Tiffany & Co., and popular chain stores. The strip is at its best around Christmas when twinkling trimmings provide welcome relief from the often gray days.

John Hancock Center ①

When this super-sleek 100-story skyscraper was built in 1970, it was the world's tallest building. Exhilarating views of Chicago **(right)** and beyond are afforded by the 94th-floor observatory and interactive viewing experience, TILT (see p79).

② Hotel InterContinental

Originally built in 1929 as a luxury club for the all-male Shrine association, this amazing hotel (see p116) reveals a range of flamboyant architectural styles in its public spaces. You can take a self-guided tour to see the highlights, including the stunning swimming pool **(below)** on the 14th floor.

③ Water Tower Place

Housing a busy shopping mall, this complex is one of the world's tallest reinforced concrete buildings. Its 100-plus shops and venues include a branch of Macy's and a Broadway-style theater.

④ The Drake Hotel

This elegant hotel (see p117) became an instant glamor hotspot when it opened on New Year's Eve in 1920. Marilyn Monroe was among the stars who visited. High tea here is a treat.

BRIDGE TO SUCCESS

The North Michigan Avenue bascule bridge, built in 1920, was the first of its kind in the world. Instrumental in Chicago's northward expansion, it provides a fitting gateway to the city's main retail artery – The Mag Mile. The southwest tower houses the McCormick Tribune Bridgehouse and River Museum (see p30), which details the history of the Chicago River and features displays on the interworkings of this landmark drawbridge.

5 Chicago Water Works and Pumping Station

Dwarfed by the surrounding skyscrapers, these structures *(see p80)* are among the few that survived the Great Fire of 1871. The water tower **(left)** contains an art gallery, and the pumping station still functions.

The Magnificent Mile Map

6 American Girl Place

Eager girls and their moms swarm to this palace of little-girlishness *(see p82)*, which stocks all kinds of merchandise from the American Girl doll range. Try the store café or attend the praised musical performance.

7 Pioneer Court

This sprawling plaza in the shadow of Tribune Tower often hosts large-scale public art exhibits. Several boat and river cruise operators set up information kiosks here, too – ideal for booking same-day and advance tours.

8 Oak Street

The north end of Mag Mile ends at Oak Street, a lane lined with high-end stores *(see p62)*. It's one of the city's most expensive retail spaces.

9 Museum of Contemporary Art Chicago

Off Michigan Avenue, the strip's cultural gem *(see p79)* features compelling temporary exhibits, a sculpture garden, and performing arts.

10 Tribune Tower

The result of a design contest organized by the *Chicago Tribune* newspaper *(see p80)*, this Gothic tower **(left)** is both adored and abhorred by locals. Either way, it's a dramatic Mag Mile landmark.

NEED TO KNOW

MAP L2–3 ■ Visitor Information: 312-409-5560 ■ "L" Station: Grand (Blue line), Chicago (Red line) ■ www.themagnificentmile.com

Water Tower Place: 835 N. Michigan Ave.; 312-440-3166; open 10am–9pm Mon–Sat & 11am–6pm Sun; www.shopwatertower.com

■ Choose from a range of high-end, global, fast food at Foodlife food court in Water Tower Place. Food is made fresh daily to eat in or to take out.

■ The Pumping Station *(see p80)* houses the main Chicago Visitor Center and a Hot Tix booth *(open 10am–6pm Tue–Sat, 11am–4pm Sun)* for reduced same-day theater tickets.

TOP 10 ⭐ Millennium Park

Designed to celebrate the turn of the 21st century with the reclamation of a former railroad yard in an industrial corner of Grant Park, Millennium Park exceeded its goals in becoming a civic magnet, at least in terms of popularity. Art, architecture, the performing arts, and nature each play a role in the popular park, which hosts free summer concerts and special events, and draws visitors year-round to its perennial attractions, led by *Cloud Gate*, its signature sculpture.

Cloud Gate Sculpture ③

Designed by sculptor Anish Kapoor, the work *Cloud Gate* (right) resembles an enlarged, reflective kidney bean, prompting its nickname, "The Bean." A selfie taken here in front of the work reflects the surrounding skyline and is Chicago's signature souvenir.

① **Crown Fountain**

Two 50-ft- (15.2-m-) high glass-block towers (above) broadcasting the videotaped faces of Chicago residents – keep watching to see if they blink – comprise the Crown Fountain by Spanish artist Jaume Plensa. In summer it's a popular splash park.

④ **Lurie Garden**

The 15-ft- (4.6-m-) high "shoulder" hedges edging the Lurie Garden pay homage to the "City of Big Shoulders" cited by Carl Sandburg in his poem *Chicago*. They shelter a delicate perennial garden that is spanned by a hardwood footbridge crossing over shallow water.

⑤ **Harris Theater**

On the northern fringe of the park, the state-of-the-art Harris Theater specializes in showcasing music and dance; some 35 Chicago performing arts companies call the Harris home, including Hubbard Street Dance, Music of the Baroque, and Chicago Opera Theater.

Jay Pritzker Pavilion ②

Designed by the architect Frank Gehry, the center-piece performing arts venue of the park is framed in flying wings of steel (right). A criss-crossing trellis of speaker-supporting steel pipes extends out over the lawn of this huge concert venue.

6 Ice-Skating Rink

The Millennium Park ice-skating rink **(left)**, generally open between December and March (weather permitting), is free, which perhaps accounts for the throngs of skaters here, eager to glide under the "The Bean."

9 Park Grill

The only restaurant in Millennium Park, Park Grill doesn't rest on its location. The quality meals provide the perfect accompaniment to the views of the city skyline, from casual burgers to more upscale fare. In warm weather, tables sprawl out onto the terrace, which serves as the skating rink in winter.

10 Millennium Monument

Anchoring the northwest corner of the park at tree-lined Wrigley Square, a semi-circular peristyle, or row of 40-ft (12-m) Doric-style columns, recall the original classical monument that stood here in the first half of the 20th century. It's now an attractive backdrop to the modern city.

Millennium Park Map

7 Nichols Bridgeway

Architect Renzo Piano, who designed the Modern Wing addition to The Art Institute of Chicago, also worked on this bridge, which gradually rises from the park to the second story of the museum across the street.

8 BP Bridge

The bridge **(below)** connecting Millennium Park to neighboring Maggie Daley Park *(see p52)* was designed by Frank Gehry. The steel-clad winding structure offers views of Lake Michigan, the skyline, and Millennium Park, and takes an intentionally indirect route.

NEED TO KNOW

MAP L4 ■ 201 E. Randolph St. ■ 312-742-1168 ■ Open 6am–11pm daily ■ www.millenniumpark.org

Welcome Center: 312-742-2963; open May–Sep: 9am–7pm; Oct–Apr: 10am–4pm

■ There are free 45-minute guided tours twice daily in May–Oct. Ask at the Welcome Center for details.

Frank Lloyd Wright's Oak Park

This suburb, 7 miles (11 km) west of downtown Chicago, contains the world's largest collection of Frank Lloyd Wright-designed buildings. It was here that Wright developed his Prairie style (inspired by the flat lines of the Midwestern plains). His work was initially considered radical compared to the typical styles of the day. Walking through Oak Park's quaint, tree-lined streets, it's evident that Wright's architecture stands out from the norm – but in all the right ways.

FRANK LLOYD WRIGHT

After moving to Oak Park in 1889, Wright (1867–1959) pioneered a unique new vision for American architecture: the Prairie style. More than a third of his life's work was produced at his Oak Park studio between 1898 and 1909. Though his personal life was wrought with scandal and he was known professionally to be particularly stubborn, Wright ultimately established himself as the first celebrity architect of international renown.

Unity Temple 2
This compact church (1908) superbly demonstrates Wright's use of poured concrete for both structural and decorative purposes **(right)**.

5 Charles Matthews House
Chicago architects Thomas Eddy Tallmadge and Vernon S. Watson designed this elegant 1909 Prairie-style residence for a wealthy pharmacist. Among the notable interior details are Prairie-inspired light fixtures and folding art-glass doors.

1 Beachy House
This impressive 1906 home contradicts many of Wright's trademarks. Instead of just stucco and wood or brick and concrete, he used them all: it also has a seven-gabled, rather than a hipped, roof.

3 Frank Lloyd Wright Home and Studio
Built when the famous architect moved to Oak Park (1889), this house **(above)** is where Wright designed over 150 structures. The children's playroom is luminous with his signature art-glass windows.

4 Pleasant Home
This 30-room Prairie-style 1897 home **(left)** built by George Maher, was Oak Park's first to have electricity. The 30-room architectural gem holds a small history museum, with exhibits relating to Tarzan creator and former local resident, Edgar Rice Burroughs.

6 Edwin Cheney House

This home sparked a tragic love affair between Wright and Mamah Cheney, leading him to abandon his family and practice. Mamah and her children were murdered at Wright's home by a servant in 1914.

7 The Bootleg Houses

Wright lost his job over these three private commissions, built while he was employed by Louis H. Sullivan (see p43). Though Queen Anne-like in style, they hint at the design elements that were to be his hallmarks.

9 Arthur Heurtley House

Wright's beautiful 1902 house (above) is absolute Prairie, with its low, wide chimney, and band of art-glass windows that makes the overhanging roof appear to float.

10 Nathan Moore House

Out of financial desperation, Wright built this charming Tudor-style home for his neighbor. After a fire destroyed the top floors in 1922, Wright's modifications echoed his West Coast concrete block houses.

NEED TO KNOW

MAP A4 ■ "L" Station: Oak Park (Green line) ■ www.gowright.org

Frank Lloyd Wright Home and Studio: 951 Chicago Ave.; 312-994-4000; open 10am–5pm daily

Unity Temple: 875 West Lake St.

Pleasant Home: 217 South Home Ave.

Arthur Heurtley House: 318 Forest Ave.

The Bootleg Houses: 1019/1027/1031 Chicago Ave.

Charles Matthews House: 432 North Kenilworth Ave.

Edwin Cheney House: 520 North East Ave.

Beachy House: 238 Forest Ave.

Nathan Moore House: 333 Forest Ave.

Harry Adams House: 710 Augusta Blvd.

■ Oak Park Visitors' Center *(1010 Lake St.)* sells maps, books, and tour tickets.

Oak Park Street Map

8 Harry Adams House

This striking 1913 home marks the last of Wright's Oak Park houses and features several of the elements that made him famous, such as exquisite stained glass, and a low overhanging roof.

The Top 10 of Everything

Stunning spiral staircase, The Rookery, S. LaSalle Street

🔟 Moments in History

1 Mid-1700s: Shikaakwa Territory

Chicago takes its name from the Indigenous Miami-Illinois word *shikaakwa*, meaning "onion." Having succeeded the Miami and Sauk and Fox peoples in the region, the Potawatomi Native American tribe staked claim to the onion-rich land in the mid-18th century.

The Great Chicago Fire of 1871

2 1871: Great Chicago Fire

More than 250 people died and 17,000 buildings were destroyed in this fire, allegedly started by a cow kicking over a lantern. Just a few buildings survived, including the Historic Water Tower and Pumping Station *(see p80)*.

3 1885: First Skyscraper

Though just a measly, by today's standards, the nine-story Home Insurance Building (now demolished), was the tallest of its time. William Le Baron Jenney achieved this architectural feat by designing the first weight-bearing steel frame. From then on, the only way to go was up.

4 1886: Haymarket Riot

Wealthy industrialists funded amazing Chicago arts institutions, but their workers toiled long hours in abominable conditions. In May 1886, a labor protest ended in an explosion at Haymarket Square that killed eight policemen and two bystanders. Eight anarchists were convicted of murder, though three were later pardoned for lack of evidence.

5 1892: First Elevated Train

The first train traveled just 3.6 miles (5.8 km) along tracks built above city-owned alleys (avoiding the need to negotiate with private property owners). By 1893, the line was extended to Jackson Park *(see p48)* to transport visitors to the World's Columbian Exposition *(see p23)*.

6 1900: Reversal of the Chicago River

With sewage flowing downriver to Lake Michigan, the source of the city's drinking water, thousands of Chicagoans were dying from the contamination. To solve the problem, engineers created a canal that forced the river to flow away from the lake: an extraordinary feat of engineering.

Chicago White Sox baseball team

7 1919: Chicago Black Sox Scandal

The Chicago White Sox was a winning baseball team but so poorly paid, that it led the players to sometimes fix the games, pocketing money from gamblers. After a group of players conspired to lose the 1919 World Series, eight of them were indicted, acquitted for insufficient evidence, but banned for life from baseball – and nicknamed the "Black Sox."

8 1929: Valentine's Day Massacre

This brutal murder of seven of Al Capone's rival gangsters is one of US history's most notorious massacres. Capone set up a sting that sent George "Bugs" Moran's main men to a nearby garage. There, Capone's henchmen, dressed as police officers, lined them up and riddled them with bullets. Seven bushes now mark the spot of the massacre (at Clark Street and Dickens Avenue).

9 1955: First McDonald's Franchise Opens

Ray Kroc, a milkshake mixer salesman, changed diets worldwide by convincing Dick and Mac McDonald to franchise their San Bernadino, California, burger stand. The original restaurant in Des Plaines – 15 miles (24 km) west of Chicago – functioned as a museum until it was demolished in early 2018.

10 2008: Barack Obama Elected President

Chicago elected its first Black mayor, Harold Washington, in 1983, but a new national barrier was vaulted with the 2008 election of Illinois senator Barack Obama as the first African American president of the United States. Thousands of jubilant voters gathered at the public rally in Grant Park on election night to celebrate the historic event. Obama was re-elected for a second term in 2012.

Barack Obama wins the 2008 election

TOP 10 CHICAGO RESIDENTS

Benny Goodman

1 Jean Baptiste Point du Sable
Chicago's first non-native settler was an African American trader, who set up camp around 1779.

2 Jane Addams
This social activist (1860–1935) founded Hull House social center *(see p97)* and won a Nobel Peace Prize.

3 Carl Sandburg
One of Chicago's nicknames, "City of the big shoulders," was penned by this author/poet (1878–1967).

4 Al Capone
This famous mobster (1899–1947) was Chicago's "Public Enemy Number One" until jailed in 1931 for tax evasion.

5 Ernest Hemingway
Born in Oak Park, this hard-living author (1899–1961) left the suburb of "wide lawns and narrow minds" at age 19.

6 Benny Goodman
Born to Russian-Jewish immigrants, jazz great Goodman (1909–1986) earned the title "King of Swing."

7 Hugh Hefner
Hefner (1926–2017) is the notorious lothario and founder of *Playboy*, whose first issue sold over 50,000 copies.

8 Curtis Mayfield
Soul musician and social activist (1942–99), Mayfield had his first hit *For Your Precious Love* at the age of 16.

9 Oprah Winfrey
Winfrey's (1954–) famous talk show was filmed in Chicago from 1984 to 2011. She is now an honorary native of the city.

10 Barack Obama
The former US President (1961–) taught at the Chicago Law School from 1992 to 2004. His residential home is in the Kenwood neighborhood.

TOP10 Skyscrapers

1 The Rookery
One of the earliest remaining skyscrapers, this 1888 landmark *(see p72)* combines traditional wall-bearing and newer steel-frame construction. The latter made it possible for its architects, Burnham and Root, to design an open interior, with offices set around a central light well.

The 100-story John Hancock Center

2 John Hancock Center
The tapering, 100-story John Hancock Center *(see p79)* is somewhat overshadowed by the higher Willis Tower but is arguably more distinctive. Designed by Skidmore, Owings & Merrill, who also did the Willis, it features its own observatory on the 94th floor.

3 Auditorium Theatre
MAP L5 ▪ 50 E. Ida B. Wells Dr
▪ For tours call 312-341-2389
Built by Adler and Sullivan in 1889, the ornate Auditorium also originally contained a hotel and office building and had one of the first public air-conditioning systems. The revamped 4,000-seat theater boasts near-perfect acoustics.

4 Reliance Building
The steel skeleton on this 1895-built skyscraper allowed it to be wrapped in glass. It offers a fine example of the Chicago window, characterized by a bay window placed between two narrow, double-hung windows *(see p74)*. Occupied by the Hotel Burnham *(see p117)* the inside has replicas of original features.

5 860–80 N. Lake Shore Drive
MAP L2
These two high-rise apartment buildings, built in 1949–51 are Chicago landmarks. They were added to the National Register of Historic Places in 1980. Architect Mies van der Rohe perfected the "less is more" approach, which many others went on to copy.

6 Willis Tower
This soaring tower, built in 1973 for retailer Sears Roebuck and Co. (who have since moved out), can be seen from almost anywhere in the city. Its Skydeck *(see pp12–13)* affords sensational views.

7 Marina City
With its twin cylindrical structures (1959–64) on the Chicago River, Marina City *(see p12)* is a "city within a city," containing offices, residences, a theater, and more. The apartments afford spectacular views, but their shape creates some interior decorating challenges.

Marina City

The innovative exterior of Aqua Tower

(8) Aqua Tower
MAP L3 = 225 N. Columbus Dr.

The exterior of the 84-story Aqua Tower appears to undulate due to the varying elevations of the skyscraper's balconies. Architect Jeanne Gang cites the striated limestone outcroppings that are common along the Great Lakes shoreline.

(9) Monadnock Building

Constructed in two stages, this Loop edifice (see p74) represents the evolution of skyscraper architecture. The northern half was built in 1891 using solely wall-bearing construction, while the southern half was built two years later and incorporated the then-emerging steel-frame technology still used today.

(10) Tribune Tower

Built in 1925, this Neo-Gothic building (see p80), with a cathedral-like buttress atop it, was the former headquarters of the Chicago Tribune. Its facade contains stones from 120 global landmarks, including China's Great Wall.

TOP 10 CHICAGO ARCHITECTS

1 William Le Baron Jenney
The "father of the skyscraper" (1832–1907) who designed the first all-metal-framed structure, the Home Insurance Building, in 1885 (see p40).

2 Daniel Burnham
Visionary city planner and architect, Burnham (1846–1912) was the man behind the White City (see p23).

3 William Holabird & Martin Roche
This influential team (Holabird 1854–1923; Roche 1853–1927) developed early Chicago-style skyscrapers including the Marquette Building (see p74).

4 Louis H. Sullivan
The creator (1856–1924) of the "form follows function" doctrine designed according to a building's intended use.

5 George Maher
A Prairie School architect (1864–1926) who favored Arts and Crafts motifs.

6 Frank Lloyd Wright
Inspired by the wide open spaces of the Midwest, Wright (see pp36–7) was the originator of the Prairie style.

7 Walter Burley Griffin
Another Prairie-style architect (1876–1937) with a namesake historic district on Chicago's South Side.

8 Ludwig Mies van der Rohe
This minimalist architect (1886–1969) was the creator of the modern glass-and-steel box.

9 Bertrand Goldberg
Goldberg (1913–1997) designed Marina City, which is typical of his curvilinear concrete shapes.

10 Jeanne Gang
Designer of the award-winning Aqua Tower, Gang (1964–) is a contemporary innovator among skyscraper designers.

Frank Lloyd Wright

TOP 10 Niche Museums

immigrants, this tiny museum's permanent collection of personal items brought over by early settlers is supplemented by temporary exhibitions on Swedish culture. The museum's interactive children's section is currently closed until further notice.

3 Hellenic Museum and Cultural Center

MAP H5 ■ 333 S. Halsted St. ■ Open 11am–5pm Tue–Fri, 11am–5pm Sat & Sun (by appt only) ■ www.national hellenicmuseum.org

Located in the city's Greektown, this museum is dedicated to celebrating Hellenic culture and the Greek immigrant experience in America.

4 National Museum of Mexican Art

MAP B5 ■ 1852 W. 19th St. ■ Open 10am–5pm Tue–Sun ■ www.national museumofmexicanart.org

The largest Latino museum in the US explores the culture *sin fronteras* (without boundaries), showing works from Mexican and Mexican-American communities. Pre-Columbian ceramics, Day of the dead candelabras, and prints by Diego Rivera are highlights of the collection.

National Museum of Mexican Art

1 National Veterans Art Museum

MAP B4 ■ 4041 N. Milwaukee Ave. ■ Open 10am–5pm Tue–Sat ■ www. nvam.org

Artwork by hundreds of veterans inspired by combat and military service is showcased in the permanent and rotating exhibitions of this small yet interesting museum.

2 Swedish American Museum

MAP B3 ■ 5211 N. Clark St. ■ Open 10am–4pm Wed–Fri, 11am–4pm Sat & Sun ■ Adm ■ www.swedish americanmuseum.org

Located in Andersonville, the historic neighborhood settled by Scandinavian

5 DuSable Museum of African American History

Named for Jean Baptiste Point du Sable, Chicago's first settler (who was of African descent) *(see p101)*, this enthralling museum chronicles

Mosaic at the DuSable Museum of African American History

the African American experience. There is a powerful exhibit on slavery, complete with shackles, while displays cover topics such as African hair art and the *Kwanzaa* holiday celebration.

6 Ukrainian Institute of Modern Art

MAP B4 ■ 2320 W. Chicago Ave. ■ Open noon–4pm Wed–Sun ■ Adm ■ www.uima-chicago.org

This tiny institute in the colorful Ukrainian Village neighborhood features rotating cultural programs, exhibitions, literary events, film screenings, and concerts. The permanent collection includes works by Chicago artists, as well as by painters and sculptors of Ukrainian descent.

Sculpture in Ukrainian Institute of Modern Art

7 International Museum of Surgical Science

MAP F4 ■ 1524 N. Lake Shore Dr. ■ Open 9:30am–5pm Mon–Fri, 10am–5pm Sat & Sun ■ Adm ■ www.imss.org

Medicine meets the macabre at this museum, of historic instruments that span 4,000 years of surgery. Murals and sculptures pay tribute to the profession. Stronger stomachs may appreciate the ancient Peruvian skulls showing evidence of early surgical attempts.

8 Mary & Leigh Block Museum of Art

MAP B2 ■ 40 Arts Circle Dr., Evanston ■ Open 10am–5pm Tue, Sat & Sun, 10am–8pm Wed–Fri ■ www.blockmuseum.northwestern.edu

This collection of paintings, drawings, and sculpture is housed in a striking glass and limestone building designed by local architect Dirk Lohan. The museum offers rotating exhibitions, as well as lectures and workshops.

9 Oriental Institute

Set in the heart of the University of Chicago campus, this museum showcases the work of the university's researchers. It houses objects found during excavations in Egypt, Nubia, Persia, Mesopotamia, Syria, Anatolia, and ancient Megiddo. There are also temporary exhibitions (see p102).

10 Jane Addams Hull-House

Nobel Peace Prize-winning social reformer Jane Addams (see p97) offered a brighter future to Chicago's immigrant population from these two Victorian houses. In addition to her original art and furniture, Hull House stages temporary exhibits relating to the social settlement that brought day care, counseling, and education to the working class.

TOP10 Film Locations

The Field Museum in *The Relic*

3 Field Museum
Scare-fest *The Relic* (1997) starred Penelope Ann Miller and Tom Sizemore as researchers trying to stop a murderous monster before it killed again. Many interior scenes were shot on replica sets but were near-perfect matches to the real museum (see pp18–19).

4 Wrigley Field
The 1914-vintage Wrigley Field (see p87), home to the Chicago Cubs, has starred in numerous baseball movies, including *The Natural*, *Rookie of the Year*, and *A League of Their Own*. It also has a cameo in *The Blues Brothers* and *Ferris Bueller's Day Off*.

5 Drake Hotel
In the film *Hero* (1992), John Bubber (Andy Garcia) dupes the public into thinking he's a hero. Feeling guilty, he resolves to jump off a window ledge at The Drake (see p117). Reality interrupted the filming when guests arrived for a party at the hotel. Director Stephen Frears protested and almost got arrested.

1 Michigan Avenue Bridge
In *Chain Reaction* (1996), Keanu Reeves is a science student at the University of Chicago (see p101) who is framed for murder. In a nail-biting chase scene, he tries to escape by running up the Michigan Avenue Bridge (see p32) as it's raised.

Michigan Avenue Bridge, featured in *Chain Reaction*

2 Daley Center and Plaza
Daley Plaza (see p75) was the setting for a chase scene in the classic cult movie *The Blues Brothers* (1980). Stars John Belushi and Dan Aykroyd, playing ex-criminal brothers, dramatically crash their car through the center's plate-glass windows, specially installed for the filming.

A scene from *Hero* in the Drake Hotel

6 Palmer House Hilton

Wrongly accused and convicted of murder, Dr. Richard Kimble (Harrison Ford) dodges the authorities led by Tommy Lee Jones to prove his innocence in *The Fugitive* (1993). He winds up in a pulse-pounding chase through this grand hotel *(see p117)* onto its roof, down its elevator shaft, and into the hotel's laundry room.

7 Randolph "L" Station
MAP L4

The "L" tracks are an apt symbol of the hard-working Chicago, and they feature significantly in the romantic comedy *While You Were Sleeping* (1995). Sandra Bullock plays an "L" station clerk who falls in love with a handsome commuter. He tumbles off the platform, Bullock saves his life, and comedy and romance ensue.

8 Wrigley Building

In *Road to Perdition* (2002) Tom Hanks is Michael Sullivan, an Irish gangster living in Chicago during the 1930s After his wife and young son are murdered, he flees town with his older son. In seeking a safe refuge, they enter a hotel, the exterior of which is the beautiful Wrigley Building *(see p33)*. However, the interior scenes were actually filmed at the Palmer House Hilton.

9 The Art Institute of Chicago

The high-school comedy *Ferris Bueller's Day Off* (1986) stars Matthew Broderick, who skips school and takes his girlfriend (Mia Sara) and best friend (Alan Ruck) on an action-packed day. At the Art Institute *(see pp14–15)*, Broderick and Sara kiss in front of a window designed by Chagall, while Ruck stares intensely at *A Sunday on La Grande Jatte* (1884).

Ferris Bueller at The Art Institute

10 Union Station
MAP J4 ■ 210 S. Canal St.

Union Station was featured in *The Untouchables* (1987). Starring Robert DeNiro as the famous gangster Al Capone and Kevin Costner as Elliot Ness, the movie is based on a true story. In an unforgettable shoot-out scene, a baby carriage falls in slow motion down the stairs and is saved at the last moment by Ness's partner.

Union Station staircase sets the scene for *The Untouchables*

🔟 Parks and Beaches

① Millennium and Grant Parks

Besides being a center for world-class art, music, architecture, and landscape design, Millennium Park offers winter ice-skating, interactive public art, alfresco dining, and free classical music concerts and film screenings (see p72). Together with the adjoining 19th-century Grant Park, which hosts many festivals (see pp66–7), it constitutes one of the finest, user-friendly green spaces in Chicago.

② North Avenue Beach

Chicago's most popular beach (see p89) attracts a broad range of urban dwellers. Its lively ocean-liner-shaped bathhouse (including shower rooms, umbrella rentals, snack vendors, and a rooftop restaurant) makes it family friendly. Beach volleyball courts and a seasonal outdoor gym are a big draw.

Volleyball at North Avenue Beach

③ Oak Street Beach
MAP L1

At the foot of the chic Gold Coast shopping lane, this beach reflects its environs. Though just next to North Avenue Beach, you won't see many children here. Oak Street is usually filled with sunbathers. The crescent-shaped strand is the closest beach to The Magnificent Mile (see pp32–3) and makes a great place to stop and dip your toes after some serious shopping.

Kid's playground, Maggie Daley Park

④ Maggie Daley Park

Maggie Daley Park (see p52) marks the northeastern boundary of Grant Park. Named for the former first lady of Chicago, the park offers a range of diversions, including a seasonal ice-skating ribbon, climbing walls, and an elaborate playground for children. There are also tennis courts, picnic tables, and a garden dedicated to cancer survivors.

⑤ Jackson Park
MAP F6

Laid out by the famed landscape designer Frederick Law Olmsted for the 1893 World's Columbian Exposition, Jackson Park, along with its Museum of Science and Industry (see pp20–21), is among the few developments still remaining from that World's Fair. The South Side park includes a Japanese garden with waterfalls, colorful lanterns, and a bird sanctuary on an island in a peaceful lagoon.

⑥ Montrose Beach
MAP C3

Chicago's largest public beach is popular with families. Great for swimming, it has a changing house and shower facilities. Other activities include volleyball, sailboat and jet ski rentals, and a large number of trails for running and biking. The vast playing fields wedged between the sand and Lake Shore Drive are the domain of Hispanic soccer clubs: on weekends their numbers draw Latin food and balloon vendors. Kayak rentals launch here in summer.

7 Washington Square
MAP K2

Located opposite the historic Newberry Library, Washington Square is a prime plot of Gold Coast for resting tired feet and gazing at the handsome 1892 building. The park's ample benches tend to draw bookish sorts and picnicking office workers at lunchtime.

8 Lincoln Park
MAP F3

The greenway Lincoln Park stretches from North Avenue up to Hollywood Avenue, a recreational apron between lakefront and housing. In Chicago's infancy, the southern portion of the park was a cemetery for Civil War dead, which were later exhumed and interred elsewhere to make way for the park. Now Lincoln Park is the North Side's counterpart to Grant Park. Attractions such as Lincoln Park Zoo (see p88), the Lincoln Park Conservatory (see p88), and Peggy Notebaert Nature Museum (see p87) supplement the beaches, harbors, playing fields, and bike paths.

South Pond Pavilion, Lincoln Park

9 Northerly Island
MAP M6

A peninsula jutting out in Lake Michigan south of the Alder Planetarium, Northerly Island is home to prairie plants, walking trails, and fountains. In summer it hosts concerts and special events at an outdoor stage that can accommodate 30,000 people on its lawn.

10 Ping Tom Memorial Park
MAP K6

Named in honor of a prominent Chinese businessman and civic leader, this green space in Chinatown features Chinese design elements and public access to the river. A boat house offers kayak rentals in summer, and the field house hosts an indoor gym and swimming pool.

📙 Off the Beaten Path

1 University of Chicago

Funded by oil magnate John D. Rockefeller (who deemed it his best-ever investment), this forward-thinking institution opened in 1892 (see p101). The university campus is home to an attractive Neo-Gothic quad, the Oriental Institute (see p102), the Smart Museum of Art, the soaring Rockefeller Memorial Chapel, and Robie House (see p102).

2 Chicago Botanic Garden

MAP A1 ▪ **1000 Lake Cook Rd., Glencoe** ▪ **Metra station: Braeside** ▪ **847-835-5440** ▪ **Open 8am–sunset daily** ▪ **www.chicago-botanic.org**

North of the city lies this lovely set of landscaped gardens, which hosts shows and special events round the year. The most popular are the Rose Garden, the Japanese Garden, and the charming English Walled Garden.

3 Evanston

MAP B2 ▪ **"L" station: Davis** ▪ **Visitors' Bureau: 847-448-4311**

This suburb brims with restaurants, galleries, and shops. Northwestern University's Mary & Leigh Block Museum of Art (see p45) and Grosse Point Lighthouse are worth a visit.

The stunning Baha'i Temple

4 Baha'i Temple

MAP A1 ▪ **100 Linden Ave., Wilmette** ▪ **"L" station: Linden Ave. (Purple line)** ▪ **847-853-2300** ▪ **Visitors' Center open mid-May–mid-Sep: 10am–8pm daily (to 5pm rest of the year); temple open 6am–10pm daily**

This exquisite white structure is one of only eight temples of the Baha'i faith worldwide. Its nine doors symbolize how people can come to God from any direction. At night, spotlights enhance its ethereal beauty and intricate design.

5 Brookfield Zoo

MAP A6 ▪ **8400 W. 31st St., Brookfield** ▪ **Metra station: Hollywood** ▪ **CTA Bus: 331** ▪ **708-688-8000** ▪ **Open 10am–5pm daily** ▪ **Adm (under-2s free)**

Over 5,900 animals live together in themed, naturalistic environments at this popular zoo. Zones include Tropic World, where thunderstorms occur regularly (you stay dry) and Habitat Africa!, whose Forest exhibit has the shy okapi and a re-created African village. In Be A Bird House, see what kind of bird you'd be on a machine that measures your flapping ability.

6 Bronzeville
MAP C5 ▪ "L" station:
35th-Bronzeville-IIT (Green line)

A bronze memorial at Martin Luther King, Jr. Drive and 35th Street honors the journey many African Americans made to this neighborhood as they fled the oppression of the South in the early 20th century. Nearby, sidewalk plaques celebrate local luminaries. Bronzeville is Chicago's answer to Harlem and offers jazz and blues in its clubs, graceful mansions aplenty, and lots of fine soul food.

7 Hemingway Birthplace
MAP A5 ▪ "L" station: Oak Park (Green line) ▪ 1-708-524-5383 ▪ Open 1–5pm Sun–Fri, 10am–5pm Sat ▪ Adm ▪ www.ehfop.org

Oak Park (see pp36–7) is well known as the first professional home of architect Frank Lloyd Wright, and for the concentration of Wright-designed buildings he left behind. But Oak Park was also home to a young Ernest Hemingway. The author's birthplace is open for tours.

8 Illinois Institute of Technology (IIT)
MAP C5 ▪ 3300 S. Federal St. ▪ "L" station: 35th-Bronzeville-IIT (Green line) ▪ 312-567-3000 ▪ Tours: www.miessociety.org/home/tours

In 1940, Ludwig Mies van der Rohe planned the campus of this new university. He also designed around 20 of the buildings, which demonstrate his design philosophies. On arrival, stop by the on-campus visitor center for information and docent- or iPod-guided tours.

Illinois Institute of Technology

9 Garfield Park Conservatory
MAP B5 ▪ 300 N. Central Park Ave. ▪ "L" station: Conservatory-Central Park Dr. (Green line) ▪ 312-746-5100 ▪ Open 9am–5pm daily (to 8pm Wed) ▪ www.garfield-conservatory.org

Beneath glass-domed roofs, flora from around the world thrives in spacious greenhouses. Information panels give the lowdown as you stroll through six indoor areas that include a Children's Garden and the Sweet House (containing plants such as cacao and sugar cane). Two grand exhibition halls host special events.

Garfield Park Conservatory

10 Pullman National Monument
MAP B6 ▪ Metra Station: Pullman/111th St. ▪ Visitors' Center: 11141 S. Cottage Grove Ave., open 11am–3pm Tue–Sun ▪ www.nps.gov/pull

Named a National Monument in 2015, this industrial town was conceived in the 1880s by railroad magnate George Pullman for his workers. The planned utopia had apartments, shops, a hospital, and a hotel, but failed after a strike in 1894, when a decrease in wages made rents unaffordable.

🔟 Chicago for Families

1 Lincoln Park Conservatory

Located in the heart of Lincoln Park's expansive swathe of green, this beautiful conservatory *(see p88)* is a haven of climate-controlled greenhouses, namely The Palm House, Orchid House, Fern Room, and Show House, all containing plant species from around the world to make up an urban jungle of sorts. It offers the perfect kid-friendly escape from the elements.

2 Maggie Daley Park

This 20-acre (8-ha) park *(see p75)*, tucked between Millennium Park and Lake Shore Drive, is a superb recreation area. The vast Play Garden for kids aged 12 and under has a pirate ship, swinging bridge, rope ladder, and Enchanted Forest with meandering paths and a rolling Wave Lawn. A seasonal ice ribbon makes a curvy path around the park's two rock climbing walls, which include routes for beginners as well as for advanced climbers. Note that for rock climbing, children must be able to wear the harnesses provided, which generally do not fit those under the age of four.

3 Chicago Children's Museum

MAP M3 ■ 700 E. Grand Ave. ■ 312-527-1000 ■ Open 10am–6pm, Fri–Sun ■ Adm ■ www.chicagochildrens museum.org

The engrossing, imaginative exhibits at this museum emphasize hands-on learning – be it digging up a dinosaur bone or designing a water channel. A central, three-story rope tunnel immediately snares the attention of older visitors, though there are age-appropriate attractions for infants to pre-teens.

Display in Chicago Children's Museum

4 Wrigley Field

A baseball-lover's park, Wrigley is a small and intimate stadium that's far less intimidating for children than many larger stadia *(see p87)*. A ticket to anywhere in the grandstand allows you to walk around and get to the rooftop terrace: the outfield stands can get rowdy, but a neighboring family section bans the beer that fuels the "bleacher bums."

5 Elevated Trains

Chicago's elevated trains (the "L") *(see p108)* provide an inexpensive roofline tour of the city. The Brown Line in particular warrants a ride from Chicago Station over the Chicago River and around the Loop, threading between the massive buildings of the financial district.

6 Chicago River Boat Tours

Even the smallest visitors will love a boat ride on the Chicago River, floating among the towering sky-scrapers and listening to stories of the city and of how the river's flow was reversed to spare Lake Michigan its pollution. Wendella and Shoreline Sightseeing *(see p115)* both embark from Michigan Avenue, and offer family-friendly narration, from spring through to fall.

7 Lincoln Park Zoo

Free admission encourages repeat visits to the Lincoln Park Zoo *(see p88)*. The zoo is a leading light for ape research, and its park setting, duck ponds, historic café, and land-mark red barn endear it to all who visit. In summer, a motorized "train" makes a scenic loop around the park, while on the pond, swan-shaped paddleboats float among the ducks.

8 John G. Shedd Aquarium

Upon arrival, head straight for the Abbott Oceanarium *(see pp28–9)* to see the beluga whales and dol-phins. Wild Reef re-creates a coral reef and houses sharks and other large predators. In the Polar Play Zone, kids can don a penguin suit and waddle in the Icy South play area or explore Arctic waters in the Icy North in a kids' size submarine. Children will also enjoy the special effects 4-D theater.

Museum of Science and Industry

9 Museum of Science and Industry

Though this museum dazzles kids and adults alike with its submarine ship and replica coal mine, it's The Idea Factory that's designed just for juniors *(see pp20–23)* With the pulling of gears and shifting of knobs, kids experiment through play with balance, construction, magnetism, and more. A current-fed waterway encourages boat building.

10 Navy Pier

Kids make a beeline for Navy Pier's traditional carnival rides *(see pp24–5)* including a 196-ft- (60-m-) high ferris wheel and musical car-ousel. The ships that line the docks, from sleek, tall-masted schooners to powerful motorboats, will also grab their attention. All the restaurants here are family friendly.

Beluga whales, Shedd Aquarium

Performing Arts

Inside the Civic Opera House

1 Lyric Opera of Chicago

Established in 1954, the Lyric Opera is among the leading companies in the US, drawing top singers and directors. From September through May it offers a mix of classical operas, modern premieres, and popular musicals. Most are performed at the ornate Art Deco Civic Opera House, with its gleaming marble floors and crystal chandeliers (see p75).

2 Court Theatre
MAP E5 ■ 5535 S. Ellis Ave.
■ www.courttheatre.org

This theater traces its roots to three Molière productions performed at the University of Chicago in 1955. The Court still mounts many classics, but it varies its seasons with musicals like *Guys and Dolls* and literary adaptations such as James Joyce's *The Dead*.

3 Chicago Symphony Orchestra

Conductor Riccardo Muti presides over the esteemed Chicago Symphony Orchestra and cellist Yo-Yo Ma is its creative consultant. The orchestra performs classical and contemporary pieces, with pop culture programs such as film scores thrown in. The orchestra's main home is the magnificent Symphony Center (see p75), but in summer they play at the outdoor suburban venue Ravinia.

4 Steppenwolf Theatre Co.

Founded in 1974 in a church basement, Steppenwolf has gained acclaim based on the fame of its ensemble, which includes actors John Malkovich and Gary Sinise (see p88). Though the company has moved to a specially built theater in Lincoln Park, it is still distinguished by raw emotion and edgy productions, and has received many notable accolades, including 12 Tony® Awards.

A performance at the Court Theatre

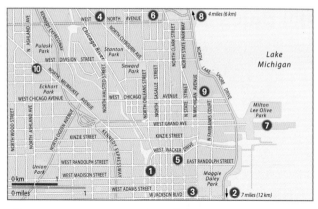

5 Goodman Theatre
MAP K3 ▪ 170 N. Dearborn St.
▪ www.goodmantheatre.org

One of Chicago's leading theater companies, the Goodman, frequently spins off productions to Broadway in New York and has earned a Tony® Award. Noted productions include dramas by Eugene O'Neill and August Wilson and an annual version of Charles Dickens' *A Christmas Carol*.

6 Second City
MAP K2 ▪ 1616 N. Wells St. ▪ www. secondcity.com

Since 1959, Chicago's famed Second City comedy troupe has launched such comic lights as Tina Fey, Amy Poehler, and Bill Murray. Reservations are a must.

Facade detail, Second City

7 Chicago Shakespeare Theater
MAP M3 ▪ 800 E. Grand Ave.
▪ www.chicagoshakes.com

This Navy Pier venue presents a dynamic space for Shakespeare's repertory. The 510-seat courtyard design is inspired by the original layout in traditional playhouses of the Bard's day. Visiting non-Shakespeare productions take over after the company's September-to-April season.

8 Old Town School of Folk Music
MAP E3 ▪ 4544 N. Lincoln Ave.
▪ www.oldtownschool.org

Since the 1950s the Old Town School has brought world and homegrown folk music performers to Chicago. Its new home in Lincoln Square opened in 1998 with a concert by Joni Mitchell, though you're more likely to catch a women's ensemble from Mali and contemporary folkies.

9 Lookingglass Theatre
MAP L2 ▪ 821 N. Michigan Ave.
▪ www.lookingglasstheatre.org

In 1988, eight Northwestern University students founded Lookingglass, a bold company incorporating dance, circus arts, and live music in its original theatrical productions. Celebrity membership (including *Friends* actor David Schwimmer) and Broadway-bound shows have furthered this company's stardom.

10 House Theatre
MAP B4 ▪ 1543 W. Division St.
▪ www.thehousetheatre.com

Though it has moved out of storefronts and into the spacious Chopin Theater, this small troop epitomizes the creativity of Chicago theater. The group frequently writes its own works, which often cover epic themes and are popular with families.

 Blues and Jazz Joints

Entrance to Rosa's

1 Rosa's
MAP E4 ▪ 3420 W. Armitage Ave. ▪ 1-773-342-0452 ▪ www.rosaslounge.com

Though off the beaten path, the family-owned Rosa's is beloved citywide for its support of local artists, such as blues harpist Sugar Blue, and for the genuine welcome extended by its owners, Tony Mangiullo and his mother Rosa. The latter sometimes cooks for the patrons of this simple tavern.

2 Kingston Mines
MAP E2 ▪ 2548 N. Halsted St. ▪ 1-773-477-4646 ▪ www.kingstonmines.com

The largest of Chicago's blues joints, Kingston Mines packs its Lincoln Park locale with students, young professionals, and a broader spectrum of tourists. Two stages provide non-stop musical entertainment from 8pm to near 4am (5am on Saturdays). Acts range from homegrown house bands to national touring headliners. The kitchen serves up beer-sopping, finger-licking barbecue food.

3 B.L.U.E.S.
MAP E2 ▪ 2519 N. Halsted St. ▪ 1-773-528-1012

Among Chicago's many blues clubs, B.L.U.E.S feels the most like a Southern juke joint. Chalk it up to the narrow confines, loud sounds, and sweaty dancers. The club is just across the street from the popular Kingston Mines, but it's a better choice for older, more musically versed blues fans. Better yet, why not stop into both!

4 House of Blues
MAP K3 ▪ 329 N. Dearborn St. ▪ 312-923-2000 ▪ www.houseofblues.com

Folk art and ornate architectural remnants festoon the funky House of Blues. The vast 1,500-seat concert hall presents a variety of national touring acts from hard rock to hip-hop in addition to blues. The Sunday gospel brunch with sittings from 9:30am to noon is a must.

5 Jazz Showcase
MAP K5 ▪ 806 S. Plymouth ▪ 312-360-0234 ▪ Open 8pm–2am Mon–Sat, 4pm–2am Sun ▪ www.jazzshowcase.com

A slick, reasonably priced jazz club that has been around since 1947, the Jazz Showcase offers some of the finest jazz in the city. Performances at this 170-seat venue are diverse, with professionals as well as bands from university music programs.

6 Andy's Jazz Club
MAP K3 ■ 11 E. Hubbard St.
■ 312-642-6805

With its musical program that begins at lunchtime and continues into the evening, Andy's fills a void for those jazz fans who can't hold out for the late-night headliners. Prime perches at the horseshoe-shaped bar are much sought after in this no-fuss River North club.

7 Green Mill Cocktail Lounge
MAP E2 ■ 4802 N. Broadway ■ 1-773-878-5552

A former Prohibition-era speakeasy, Uptown's landmark Green Mill is a vintage treasure with a sweeping curved bar, vinyl booths, fading murals, and an authentic air of Chicago's gangster past. The city's premier jazz talents like Kurt Elling and Patricia Barber regularly play gigs here and Uptown Poetry Slam features every Sunday. It's out of the way but every cabbie in the city knows how to get there.

Buddy Guy headlining at his club

9 Buddy Guy's Legends
MAP L5 ■ 700 S. Wabash Ave.
■ 312-427-1190

A legend himself, bluesman Buddy Guy operates perhaps the best blues club in the city. The popular South Loop destination draws a mix of students, tourists, and local fans, particularly when Guy himself headlines (see p98).

10 California Clipper
1002 N. California Ave. ■ 1-773-384-2547 ■ www.californiaclipper.com

Home of the Purple Martini, this restored retro club, with a 40-ft (12-m) wooden bar and red-leather booths, bills itself as "the only bar with grape soda on its gun." Catch local, live country, dance, jazz, and blues from Thursday through Sunday (Monday is bingo night). See if you can spot "The Woman in White," the Clipper's elegant 1940s ghost.

Green Mill Cocktail Lounge

8 Blue Chicago
MAP K2 ■ 536 N. Clark St. & 736 N. Clark St. ■ 312-661-0100 ■ Open 8pm–1:30am Mon–Fri & Sun (to 2:30am Sat) ■ www.bluechicago.com

Popular with tourists, Blue Chicago in River North operates two clubs located two blocks apart. Seats at both venues are few and far between, so come early if you need one, or be prepared to dance. The admission charge covers both clubs, which encourages bar hopping.

Retro-style interior, California Clipper

🔟 Bars and Clubs

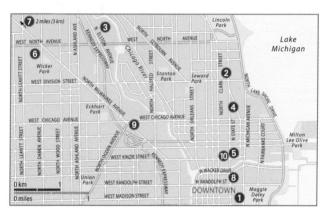

1 Cindy's

On the rooftop of the Chicago Athletic Association Hotel, the stylish, glass-roofed Cindy's *(see p77)* feels like a garden party from opening hours to close. A terrace with two firepits offers panoramic views of Millennium and Grant parks, and Lake Michigan. Cocktail choices include large-format dispensers designed for sharing.

A night out at the Zebra Lounge

2 Zebra Lounge

An illegal speakeasy during Prohibition, this tiny piano bar has stood the test of time and competition, packing in loyal revelers nightly. Zebra prints dominate the decor, and martinis are the drink of choice. Singing along with the pianist to show tunes, torch songs, and old songs is expected.

3 Hideout

MAP D4 ■ 1354 W. Wabansia Ave. ■ 1-773-227-4433

Located off an industrial corridor on the Northside, Hideout is a popular destination for live music and arty performances. Many big names played here when they were rising stars, including Andrew Bird, and they often return. Events such as the Write Club pit debating scribes against one another.

4 Le Bar

MAP K2 ■ 20 E. Chestnut St. ■ 312-324-4000

In the beautiful Sofitel Hotel *(see p116)*, a fashionable, over-30, mixed crowd fills this lobby lounge after work, lingering until the wee hours of the morning. Servers clad in black dispense martinis with scrumptious flavors such as chocolate and raspberry, and can cater to all tastes.

5 Sable Kitchen & Bar

MAP K3 ■ 505 N. State St. ■ 312-755-9704 ■ Opening times vary

Named after Chicago's first non-native settler, Jean Baptiste Point du Sable *(see p41)*, this dimly lit restaurant has a classic 1940s vibe to it. With its quintessential American dishes, interesting vegetarian options and an extensive appetizer list (which includes a range of delicious soups), Sable Kitchen & Bar is great for a lavish meal out.

6 The Violet Hour
MAP B4 ▪ 1520 N. Damen Ave. ▪ 1-773-252-1500

No sign marks the sophisticated Violet Hour in Wicker Park, a drape-swagged room that is Chicago's original artisan bar. Hostesses seat guests and waiting in line is common, but once ensconced in the exclusive high-backed chairs or booths, this is a great place to savor craft cocktails and lively conversations.

7 Billy Sunday
MAP B4 ▪ 3143 W. Logan Blvd. ▪ 1-773-661-2485

Chef Mathias Merges runs this upscale cocktail-focused bar located in Logan Square. If you're not familiar with bergamot bitters, Fernet or rhum agricole, it's best to quiz the creative mixologist. The bar also offers its own bottled and carbonated boozy sodas. A food menu of snacks and small plates keeps hunger pangs at bay.

8 Roof on the Wit
MAP K2 ▪ 201 N. State St. ▪ 312-239-9501 ▪ Closed Sun

Nestled amid the skyscrapers of the Loop, with spectacular views of the city, the winding "L", the Chicago River, and Lake Michigan, the Wit is a chic complex of lounge bars. Snuggle

by an open fire and take in the ultra-hip ambience and stunning vistas, with a cocktail in hand.

9 Matchbox
MAP B4 ▪ 770 N. Milwaukee Ave. ▪ 312-666-9292

Named for its tiny footprint, this cocktail bar has been a local favorite since the 1940s. Stop by and order a flawless martini, fresh-juice gimlet, or a timeless Tom Collins: the bartenders here know their classics.

Subterranean Three Dots and a Dash

10 Three Dots and a Dash
MAP K3 ▪ 35 N. Clark St. ▪ 312-610-4220

To find this hideaway, enter through the alley and descend to another time and place. Occupying several intimate rooms, this tiki bar includes a grass-thatch-fringed area serving pineapple-and-orchid-garnished drinks in classic tiki cups. Mai Tais and other cocktails pair well with *pupu platters* (island-style bar snacks).

Roof on the Wit, providing rooftop views over the city

⟨TOP 10⟩ Places to Eat

① Girl & the Goat
Popular chef Stephanie Izard is the girl in Girl & the Goat *(see p77)*. Though she offers goat and other bold-flavored dishes, there is a particular emphasis on vegetables, which make up a third of the menu. Reserve a table well in advance, or try your luck and arrive at the opening time (4:30pm).

② Alinea
Considered to be one of the world's foremost restaurants, Alinea has three Michelin stars and offers an exceptional gourmet experience *(see p93)*. Chef Grant Achatz prepares tasting menus of highly creative New American dishes with wine or non-alcoholic pairings, served in three elegant dining areas with modern white and grey decor. The service is impeccable. Reserve well in advance.

③ Lou Mitchell's
A classic diner *(see p77)* in the Loop where the waitresses call you "Honey" and the coffee is bottomless, Lou Mitchell's has been around since 1923. Its trek-worthy meal is breakfast, highlighted by double-yolk eggs and homemade hash browns served in a skillet. Tables turn quickly and the staff doles out free donuts and

The retro Lou Mitchell's diner

candy with good cheer to those waiting in line. Women and kids are greeted with Milk Duds when they enter the restaurant.

④ North Pond
Hidden from the road in Lincoln Park and overlooking the splendid Chicago skyline, North Pond is a treasure – once you find it *(see p93)*. Originally built in 1912 and lodged in an Arts-and-Crafts-style building, the café offers an American seasonal menu with an emphasis on produce sourced from the Midwest. Though dinner is the star, lunches of sandwiches, soups, and salads are equally creative as well as very well presented.

⑤ The Purple Pig
This Chicago favourite *(see p83)*, primely located along The Magnificent Mile, has been serving acclaimed Mediterranean-inspired dishes since it opened in 2009. It features a meat-heavy menu (the roasted bone marrow and crispy pig's ear are the standouts), with a few delicious veggie dishes as well. A wine pairing is suggested for every menu item.

⑥ Pizzeria Uno
Established in 1943, this Victorian brownstone restaurant *(see p77)* has been baking deep-dish

Pizzeria Uno, a Chicago institution

pizzas for as long as Chicagoans have been debating on who serves the best pie. The pizza filled with cheese and toppings of your choice, is a meal in one slice. Often due to the strain of demand, orders are sent up the street to its spin-off Pizzeria Due. Uno's individual pizza served at lunchtime is a real bargain.

7 Next
Founded by acclaimed chef Grant Achatz, Next (see p83) reinvents itself each quarter with a new themed menu. Previous transformations include Paris Circa 1900, Childhood Memories, and Modern Chinese. Bookings are only sold through an advance ticketing system and sell out quickly, though resale options are often posted online.

8 Gibson's Steakhouse
Boisterous and convivial, Gibson's Steakhouse (see p83) exudes a good time. A regular crowd of politicians, sports figures, and conventioneers packs the place nightly. The steakhouse fare is

in every way a match to the atmosphere – big and bold. Huge lobster tails vie for attention with large slabs of beef. A reservation is critical, but for a more casual, walk-in experience, try the burgers next door at Hugo's Frog Bar.

9 Avec
Chicagoans have long been enamored with Avec (see p77), a fine dining restaurant whose intimate and minimalist wood-paneled interior is as cozy as a sauna. Focusing on Mediterranean-inspired bites and entrees, Chef Paul Kahan repeatedly earns accolades for Avec's take on delectable shared plates and an incredible list of regional wines.

10 Frontera Grill
Chef Rick Bayless' and his wife, Deann Groen Bayless's vacation in Mexico inspired them to come up with Frontera Grill, a popular restaurant credited with bringing authentic regional Mexican food – rather than the Tex-Mex taco fare – stateside (see p83). As seen in the colorful kitchens of Mexico, chili-roasted salsas and rich *moles* accompany grilled meats and delicious seafood. Since reservations are only available for parties of more than six, seats in the folk art-filled room go early as smaller groups try to avoid disappointment.

📖10 Shopping Destinations

1 State Street

A slew of chain stores line this legendary street *(see p73)*, but it's the neighborhood's old-time department store that makes it unique. The former Marshall Field's, now Macy's *(see p76)*, here since 1907, satisfies every wealthy shopper's needs. At TJ Maxx the prices are lower, but the variety is still extensive *(see p76)*.

Inside Macy's, State Street

2 Oak Street

MAP L1 ■ Borders: N. Michigan Ave. & Rush St.

If you have to ask how much it costs, you should probably plan on just window-shopping along this stretch of Chicago's upper-crust Gold Coast. Boutiques here sell designer wear, accessories, and shoes fit for a Paris runway – and include some shops exclusive to Chicago such as Tessuti (menswear) and Designs by Ming (custom clothing design).

3 Andersonville

MAP B3 ■ Clark St. between Foster and Bryn Mawr

This far Northside neighborhood hosts a string of independent boutiques along the bustling Clark Street. Zoning regulations have kept out big-box stores with the result that the bookshops, galleries, design stores, and clothing specialists offer unique goods.

4 Bucktown Neighborhood

MAP B4 ■ Borders: Fullerton Ave. to Division Ave. & Kennedy Expressway to Western Ave.

Once a hotspot for starving artists, Bucktown and the adjacent Wicker Park are now gentrified locales brimming with clothing stores, edgy music shops, high-style designer boutiques, and athleisure brands.

5 Bloomingdale's Home and Furniture Store

MAP K3 ■ 600 N. Wabash Ave. ■ Opening times vary

This store's lovingly restored 1913 Moorish-style building is an attraction in its own right. Inside, there's a sleek, four-level atrium with home decor departments that sell everything from bedding to furniture.

6 Broadway Antique Market

MAP E2 ■ 6130 N. Broadway ■ Open 11am–7pm Mon–Sat, 11am–6pm Sun

An old-time movie palace sign indicates the 1939 building that houses this market. With 85 dealers stocking artwork, jewelry, clothing, and more in styles such as Arts and Crafts, Art Deco, and Mid-Century Modern, you are sure to find something to suit.

Broadway Antique Market

7 The Magnificent Mile

This stretch of North Michigan Avenue is one of the world's retail meccas *(see pp32–3)*. Besides sophisticated designer boutiques, there are malls (each with high-end department stores); and big-name chain and flagship stores.

Retail heaven, The Magnificent Mile

8 Architectural Artifacts

MAP B3 ▪ 4325 N. Ravenswood Ave. ▪ Open 10am–5pm daily

This sprawling warehouse on the Northside is chock-full of architectural and antique cast-offs, many from demolished buildings. Wares come from Chicago, Europe, and South America and range from massive stone mantles to neon signs and ceramic art tiles.

9 CAC Store

MAP L3 ▪ 111 E. Wacker Dr. ▪ Open 10am–5pm daily

The CAC Store is housed inside the main building of the Chicago Architecture Center (formerly the Chicago Architecture Foundation), which also puts on exhibitions and runs city tours *(see p31)*. Browse the shop for architecture and design-related books, art-glass panels and lamps in Frank Lloyd Wright designs, desk gadgets, desirable kitchen gizmos, jewelry, clothing, posters and prints, and other souvenirs.

10 Armitage Avenue

This tree-lined street in Lincoln Park *(see p49)* is a favorite for those who are seeking out-of-the-ordinary clothing, home decor, bath and body products – and don't mind spending more to get it.

TOP 10 CHICAGO SOUVENIRS

1 Frango Mints
Marshall Field's/Macy's *(see p76)* doesn't make these delicious mint chocolates anymore, but still sells them by the box-full.

2 Blues & Jazz Albums
Albums by Chicago music legends are on sale at the Water Works Visitor Information Center *(see p80)*.

3 Vosges Haut Chocolat
Exotic velvety truffles with global flavors are on offer here.

4 Art Poster
See the real thing, then buy a copy at The Art Institute of Chicago's extensive gift shop *(see p14)*.

5 Chicago Snowglobe
Recall Chicago winters with a city skyline snowglobe from Accent Chicago in the Water Tower Place mall *(see p32)*.

6 Cubs Baseball Cap
Head to the Cubs Team Store *(668 N. Michigan Ave)* for caps of the Major League team *(see p87)*.

7 Art Glass
Take home a little bit of Prairie style with a replica of the Frank Lloyd Wright art-glass panel from the CAC (Chicago Architecture Center) Store.

8 Garrett's Popcorn
Garrett's Popcorn, especially the signature cheddar-caramel mix, is a classic guilty pleasure in the city.

9 Sue Skeleton Model
Sue, one of the world's largest *T. rex* skeletons is far less menacing in a mini model form from the Field Museum *(see p18)*.

10 Sports Jersey
Merchandise such as club T-shirts, Blackhawks sweaters, and Bulls jerseys make very popular apparel purchases.

Chicago Blackhawks jersey

TOP 10 Chicago for Free

1 Navy Pier
Navy Pier offers some of the most scenic strolls in Chicago *(see pp24–5)*. The pier is carnival-like, with myriad attractions begging you to spend money. The entry and the fireworks displays on Wednesday and Saturday nights during the summer, are free.

2 Lincoln Park Zoo
Lincoln Park Zoo is one of the last free zoos in the country *(see p88)*. Home to more than 1,000 mammals, reptiles, and birds, it is a leader in wildlife conservation with efforts toward saving endangered species.

3 Public Art
Many famous artists, such as Pablo Picasso, Alexander Calder, and Marc Chagall have left their artistic mark on the city. Details of public art downtown are included in the Loop Sculpture Guide, downloadable from www.cityofchicago.org.

4 Lakefront Recreational Path
The 18-mile (29-km) paved path that runs along Lake Michigan is popular for running, cycling, skating, and walking. Many hotels offer rental bicycles and the city's bike-share program Divvy *(see side bar)* offers cheap wheels.

Blues festival for free at Grant Park

5 Free Events
Mayor's Office of Special Events (recorded info): 312-744-3370 ▪ www.cityofchicago.org/specialevents
Summer in Chicago brings lots of free outdoor festivals, from the big music events of Grant Park, such as the Chicago Blues Festival *(see p66)*, to parades, circuses in the parks, and neighborhood festivals that feature entertainment and vendors.

6 Comedy Shows
Comedy Sportz: 929 W. Belmont St.; 1-773-549-8080; www.comedysportzchicago.com ▪ iO Theater: 3541 N. Clark St.; 1-773-880-0199; www.ioimprov.com/chicago
Chicago is the place to catch the best rising comedy and improv stars. The iO Theater runs dozens of shows each week from its Lincoln Park

Lakefront Recreational Path, great for strolling or cycling

headquarters, some of them free and all of them a blast. Also check Comedy Sportz for freebies.

7 Brewery Tours

Lagunitas Brewing: 2607 W. 17th St.; 1-773-522-2097; www. lagunitas.com ■ **Revolution Brewing:** 2323 N. Milwaukee Ave.; 1-773-227-2739; www.revbrew.com

Several microbreweries offer free tours of their facilities, including the sprawling Lagunitas Brewing in Pilsen. Tours begin in a recreation room with generous free samples, pinball machines, and other old-time amusements. Revolution Brewing in Logan Square also offers guided tours Wednesday to Sunday.

8 Free Museums

It's a good idea to seek out the smaller museums that offer free admission, including the National Museum of Mexican Art (see p44).

Millennium Park drawing a crowd

9 Millennium Park Programming

Over the summer, the Millennium Park (see pp34–5) hosts a series of free events and performances, ranging from concerts by the Lyric Opera (see p54) and Chicago Children's Choir to screenings of popular movies.

10 Free Tours

The tourism bureau Choose Chicago (see p113) offers free guided tours led by locals. Sign up 10 days in advance via the website for a Chicago Greeter tour running for 2 to 4 hours. If you haven't planned ahead, InstaGreeters (see p114) are available for 1-hour tours Friday to Sunday.

TOP 10 MONEY-SAVING TIPS

Chicago's popular Divvy bikes

1 See the city on a Divvy Bike. A short ride of 30 mins costs $3. Get a day pass for $15 and take 3-hour rides within 24 hrs.; www.divvybikes.com.

2 Many restaurants have good-value "Early Bird Specials" or pre-theater menus. Look for signs throughout the city advertising these deals.

3 Chicago's many beautiful parks offer free skating rinks, beaches, pools, tennis courts, and walking and cycling paths.

4 Choose Chicago offers several promotions, such as Winter Delights, which include discounts on lodging, attractions, and meals; www. choosechicago.com.

5 CityPass grants entry to five top attractions including the Shedd Aquarium and Field Museum for 50 percent off; www.citypass.com.

6 Purchase half-price tickets for same-day theater performances at three Hot Tix booths. See www.hottix. org for shows available.

7 Ring the Loop aboard the Brown Line "L" running out to Lincoln Park and back again for a scenic tour at just $2.50 (see pp108–9).

8 Look for neighborhood restaurants that lack a liquor license and allow diners to bring their own beer or wine.

9 Skip the observatory at the John Hancock Center (see p79) and hit its 95th-floor Signature Lounge for equivalent views.

10 Visit the Chicago Cultural Center to see its stained-glass domes and to catch some of the free concerts that are regularly scheduled here (see p71).

🔟 Festivals and Events

① Chicago Blues Festival
MAP L6 ■ Late May–early Jun

The raucous weekend-long Blues Festival kicks off summer in Chicago. About 750,000 listeners converge on Grant Park for the world's largest free blues event. The main stage hosts traditional blues and gospel performers like Mavis Staples, jazz interpreters such as Mose Allison, and blues-inflected artists like Bonnie Raitt. Smaller side stages offer a more intimate experience.

② Lollapalooza
MAP L6 ■ Late Jul ■ www.lollapalooza.com

The three-day rock festival known as Lollapalooza takes over Grant Park in late July. Major headliners such as Paul McCartney and Florence + the Machine are joined by emerging rockers, DJs, and techno innovators over several stages across the park. Passes go on sale, and usually sell out, in March.

③ Chicago Air and Water Show
312-744-3316 ■ Mid-Aug

This display of military power features historic aircraft flybys, a staged amphibious attack, and precision flying teams. Prime viewing spots are from Oak Street to Montrose Beach.

Chicago Jazz Festival

④ Chicago Jazz Festival
MAP L6 ■ 312-744-3316 ■ Late Aug/early Sep (inc. Labor Day weekend)

The Jazz Fest caps summer, when music fans are drawn to Grant Park for free concerts by greats like Branford Marsalis and Roy Hargrove.

⑤ Chicago Gospel Music Festival
MAP L6 ■ 312-744-3316 ■ Early Jun ■ www.choosechicago.com

For three days, Grant Park resounds with stirring choirs and impassioned soloists. Headliners have included soul singer Al Green.

⑥ World Music Festival
312-744-3315 ■ Mid-Sep ■ www.worldmusicfestivalchicago.org

This city-wide, multi-venue, week-long festival showcases the very best

Chicago Air and Water Show

of traditional and contemporary international music. Concerts are low-cost or even free.

⑦ The Magnificent Mile Holiday Lights Festival

MAP L2 ■ Mid-Nov–end Dec

Merchants mark the start of the holiday season by lighting the shops, lampposts, and trees along Michigan Avenue. The parade and fireworks above the Chicago River on the Saturday night before Thanksgiving warrant braving the inevitable chill.

⑧ Taste of Chicago

MAP L6 ■ Grant Park
■ 312-744-3316 ■ Late Jun–early Jul

Chicago's signature foods are featured during the nearly two-week-long Taste of Chicago. Musical entertainers, a carnival with rides, and cooking demonstrations happen at the sprawling Grant Park event.

Entrance to Taste of Chicago

⑨ Old Town Art Fair

MAP F4 ■ 1763 N. Park Ave.
■ 312-337-1938 ■ Jun ■ www.old townartfair.org

This 50-year-old fair installs 250 artist booths along Old Town's lanes. There are also food vendors, kids' entertainment, and garden tours.

⑩ Chicago Summer Neighborhood Festivals

312-744-3316 ■ May–Sep ■ www. choosechicago.com

Chicago has upwards of 100 neighborhood festivals. Virtually every summer weekend features an event or three, ranging from the North Halsted Market Days to the ethnic Korean Street Festival.

TOP 10 SPORTS TEAMS AND EVENTS

Chicago Bears in action

1 Chicago Bears
Sep–Dec ■ www.chicagobears.com
The football team generates raucous fans and tailgate picnics when in action on Soldier Field (see p12).

2 Chicago White Sox
Apr–Sep ■ www.whitesox.com
The White Sox are renowned for their top-quality baseball.

3 Chicago Cubs
The baseball games of the 2017 Series champions at the Wrigley Field are often sell-outs (see p87).

4 Chicago Bulls
Oct–Apr ■ www.bulls.com
Their basketball hasn't been the same since superstar Michael Jordan left.

5 Chicago Blackhawks
Oct–Apr ■ www.chicago blackhawks.com
The Stanley Cup-winning NHL ice hockey team shares the United Center (see p13) with the Bulls.

6 Arlington Park
May–Sep ■ www.arlingtonpark.com
Thoroughbred horses race at this park just north of Chicago.

7 Chicago Fire
Apr–Oct ■ www.chicago-fire.com
Many local soccer fans support the Fire.

8 Chicago Wolves
Oct–May ■ www.chicagowolves.com
Four-time league champions offer a great evening of hockey.

9 Chicago Marathon
Oct ■ www.chicagomarathon.com
45,000 entrants run through the city.

10 Chicago Triathlon
Aug ■ www.chicagotriathlon.com
Over 6,000 run, bike, and swim in this action-packed one-dayer.

Chicago
Area by Area

Chicago's Gold Coast area fringed by Oak Street Beach

TOP10 The Loop

Named for the ring of elevated train tracks that encircle it, this is downtown Chicago's core, and the city's financial and governmental hub. Abuzz with laptop-toting business folk during the week, the Loop is transformed on weekends when a veritable shopping frenzy erupts along its famous State Street. Those thirsty for culture come flocking to see the collections of The Art Institute of Chicago and to view the area's many architecturally significant buildings and its notable public art, while public parks offer green recreational spaces and the Riverwalk pedestrian path is a great place for strolling. The vibrant theater district, with its variety of shows, and the many great bars and restaurants give the area a lively nightlife.

Lion statue, The Art Institute of Chicago

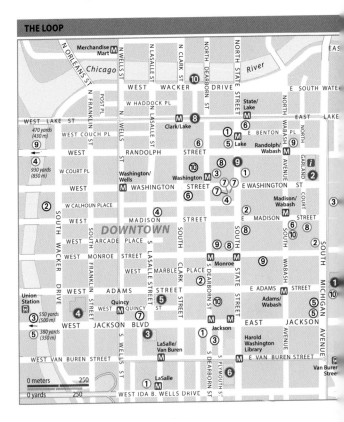

1 The Art Institute of Chicago

This extraordinary collection spans over 4,000 years of international art (see pp14–15), much of it donated by wealthy Chicago collectors.

2 Chicago Cultural Center

MAP L4 ■ 78 E. Washington St. ■ 312-744-6630 ■ Open 10am–7pm Mon–Fri, 10am–5pm Sat & Sun ■ Tours 1:15pm Wed, Fri & Sat ■ www.chicagoculturalcenter.org

Built in 1897 as the city's first main library, this magnificent Beaux-Arts building was described at the time as the "people's palace." In 1991, the library moved out, allowing several galleries, performance spaces and a visitor information center to move in. Guided tours offer a historical

Tiffany Dome, Chicago Cultural Center

overview of the building, which occupies an entire block and has one of the world's largest domes, designed by L. C. Tiffany, and rooms modeled after the Doge's Palace in Venice and the Acropolis in Athens.

3 Chicago Board of Trade

MAP K5 ■ 141 W. Jackson Blvd.

The Chicago Board of Trade (CBOT) was founded in 1848 to create a central marketplace in the fast-developing city, and moved to its current 45-story home in 1930. Designed by Holabird and Root, it is a stunning example of Art Deco. Capping the limestone building is a huge statue of Ceres, the Roman goddess of grain and harvest. A 23-story glass-and-steel addition designed by Helmut Jahn was added in 1980. Tours of the building are available via the Chicago Architecture Center (see p31).

4 Willis Tower

An architectural superlative, the tower offers breathtaking views from its 103rd-floor Skydeck (see pp12–13), where you'll find yourself on top of 222,500 tons of steel.

Willis Tower

① **Top 10 Sights**
see pp71–3

① **Places to Eat and Drink** see p77

① **Shops**
see p76

① **Architectural Sights**
see p74

① **The Best of the Rest**
see p75

WACKER DRIVE
NORTH STETSON AVE
NORTH COLUMBUS DRIVE
ST STETSON AVE
NORTH STREET
Millennium Station
Maggie Daley Park ④
❼ Millennium Park
Monroe Harbor
EAST MONROE DRIVE
SOUTH LAKE SHORE DRIVE
SOUTH COLUMBUS DRIVE
Chicago Harbor
DRIVE
❼ Grant Park

5 The Rookery

MAP K4 ■ 209 S. LaSalle St. ■ Open 6am–6pm Mon–Fri (to 2pm Sat), closed Sun

This 11-story building, with its rusticated red granite base, was the country's largest office building and a precursor to modern skyscrapers when it was completed in 1888 by Burnham and Root (see p43). Its stunning light court was redesigned in 1907 by Frank Lloyd Wright (see pp36–7), who added a grand staircase and hanging light fixtures, both of which carry his signature circle-in-square motif.

The Rookery's splendid light court

6 Harold Washington Library Center

MAP K5 ■ 400 S. State St. ■ Open 9am–9pm Mon–Thu, 9am–5pm Fri & Sat, 1–5pm Sun

Named after former city Mayor Harold Washington, Chicago's first African American mayor, this is the largest public library building in the country. Its collections, which include a superlative Blues Archive and a vast children's library, fill an incredible 70 miles (110 km) of shelving. Architects Hammond, Beeby, and Babka incorporated architectural elements of several Chicago landmarks, such as The Rookery and The Art Institute of Chicago (see pp14–15) in the building's design: don't miss the ninth-floor Winter Garden atrium, which soars two stories to a spectacular glass dome.

Elevated train, the Loop

THE LOOP'S SCULPTURE

Setting a trend for public artwork downtown, Pablo Picasso's untitled sculpture, simply known as "the Picasso," was donated to Chicago in 1967. The Loop's street corners now feature more than 100 sculptures, mosaics, and murals by established as well as upcoming artists. A guide to the open-air artworks can be downloaded from www.cityofchicago.org.

7 Millennium and Grant Parks

The modern Millennium Park (see pp34–5) is Chicago's superb adaptation of its "front yard." The park is home to a dynamic Frank Gehry–designed music pavilion and pedestrian bridge, and a vast sculpture, Cloud Gate (aka "The Bean"), by British artist Anish Kapoor. It also boasts lush gardens, restaurants, a winter ice rink, peristyle, and an interactive fountain by Spanish artist Jaume Plensa. The adjoining Grant Park (see p48) hosts many summer festivals including the Taste of Chicago (see p67). It is also home to Museum Campus (see p94), The Art Institute of Chicago (see pp14–17), and the ornate 1927 Buckingham Fountain.

8 The "L"

Originally called the Union Loop, this system of elevated trains came about after the 1871 Great Chicago Fire (see p40) when the city was rebuilt with such unexpected success that, within 20 years, its streets could no longer handle the influx of people, streetcars, and horses filling them. Today, four lines ring the business district – the

Orange, Purple, Pink, and Brown lines (see p52)– with three others connecting it to places farther afield.

9 State Street

MAP K4 ■ From Wacker Dr. to Ida B. Wells Dr.

This "great street" got its nickname from the 1922 hit song Chicago. Although it didn't always live up to this catchy moniker, it has won back many fans since its face-lift in 1996. It now sports replica Art Deco lampposts and subway entrances, and was listed on the National Register of Historic Places in 1998. This dynamic stretch has shopping, history, education, architecture, theater, and dining. The atmosphere is especially merry when the Thanksgiving parade brings Santa to town.

Enjoying the sunshine, Riverwalk

10 Chicago Riverwalk

Running along the south bank of the Chicago River, beginning near Lake Michigan, the Chicago Riverwalk (see pp30–31) is a waterside walkway that weaves under bridges. The pedestrian and bike path is a great place for spying the skyscrapers that line the river, and for picnicking. There are also restaurants, cafés, a floating garden, and boat and bike rentals. The section from State to LaSalle has amphitheater-like seating and an area for kayak launches.

A DAY IN THE LOOP

▶ **MORNING**

Start early with breakfast at the **Cherry Circle Room** (see p77), off the lobby of the historic **Chicago Athletic Association** hotel (see p117). Stroll across the street to **Millennium Park** (see pp34–5), to see the *Cloud Gate* sculpture, the video-screen fountains, and the Lurie Garden. From the park, take the pedestrian bridge designed by Renzo Piano, directly to **The Art Institute of Chicago** (see p71). A whirlwind tour of the highlights, located on the upper level and in the Modern Wing, takes a couple of hours. Have lunch at **Terzo Piano** (see p77), on the 3rd floor of the Modern Wing, and enjoy panoramic views of Michigan Avenue and the the city's skyline.

AFTERNOON

Walk up nearby **State Street**, stopping to browse the shops, until you reach the Chicago River. Spend an hour or two meandering along the **Chicago Riverwalk**. Be sure to stop by the **Chicago Architecture Center**, which has a lovely shop (see p63) stocked with design-related souvenirs.

EVENING

Book a pre-theater table at **Petterino's** (see p77), an old-school supper club, then check out the show at the **Goodman Theatre** (see p55) next door. Head back to the Chicago Athletic Association for a nightcap at **Cindy's** (see p77) rooftop bar.

See map on pp70–71 ◀

Architectural Sights

1 Monadnock Building
MAP K5 ▪ 53 W. Jackson Blvd.

At 16 stories (see p43), this impressive Holabird and Roche designed building (1891) is one of the world's tallest all-masonry high-rises. Inside, there's a magnificent wrought-iron staircase.

2 Marquette Building
MAP K4 ▪ 56 W. Adam St.

Chicago architects Holabird and Roche built this Chicago School structure with a steel skeleton and decorative ornamentation in 1895.

3 Fisher Building
MAP K5 ▪ 343 S. Dearborn St.

A Chicago School edifice with a steel structure, this 1896 Neo-Gothic building is by Daniel H. Burnham. Aquatic motifs on the façade honor the building's first owner, L. G. Fisher.

Art Deco features, One North LaSalle

4 One North LaSalle
MAP K4

This 1930-built, 49-story building was Chicago's tallest for 35 years, and is one of the city's best surviving examples of Art Deco architecture.

5 Santa Fe Center
MAP L6

Beaux-Arts architect Daniel H. Burnham designed this elegant high-rise in 1904. Its carved building signs are from Chicago's days as a railroad hub.

Beaux-Arts-style Chicago Theatre

6 Chicago Theatre
MAP K4 ▪ 175 N. State St.

The red sign of this Beaux-Arts-style theater is a symbol of Chicago. Built in 1921 as a movie theater, today it is a performance venue.

7 Reliance Building
MAP K4 ▪ 1 W. Washington St.

Daniel H. Burnham's stunning glass-and-white-glazed-terra-cotta building (1895) (see p117) is now the Alise Chicago hotel.

8 Sullivan Center
MAP K4 ▪ 1 S. State St.

Eye-catching cast-iron swirls on part of the exterior of this building (1899 and 1903) express architect Louis H. Sullivan's love of elaborate detail.

9 Inland Steel Building
MAP K4 ▪ 30 W. Monroe St.

One of the first skyscrapers to be built (in 1957) on steel, not concrete, pilings, this predates the John Hancock Center (see p12) in using external supports.

10 Federal Center
MAP K4 ▪ 219 S. Dearborn St.

Flanked by Ludwig Mies van der Rohe's Modernist federal buildings, this plaza (1959–74) contains Alexander Calder's striking steel statue Flamingo (1974).

See map on pp70–71

The Best of the Rest

1 **Loop Theater District**
MAP K4

A sidewalk plaque at Randolph and State streets denotes Chicago's officially designated Theater District, a cluster of old and new theaters.

2 **Civic Opera House**
MAP J4 ■ 20 N. Wacker Dr.
■ www.lyricopera.org

This 1929 structure (see p54) was inspired by Paris's Opera Garnier. It is home to the Lyric Opera of Chicago.

3 **Old St. Patrick's Church**
MAP J4 ■ 700 W. Adams St.

Chicago's oldest church (1856) is crowned by two towers – one Romanesque, one Byzantine – symbolizing East and West.

4 **Maggie Daley Park**
MAP L4 ■ 37 E. Randolph St.

If Millennium Park is about art, its neighbor just to the east is all about play. Features include an elaborate children's playground, two climbing walls, tennis courts, and a popular frozen skating ribbon in winter.

5 **Symphony Center**
MAP L4 ■ 220 S. Michigan Ave. ■ www.cso.org

At the heart of this center (see p54) is Orchestra Hall (1904), the stunning home of the Chicago Symphony Orchestra.

Orchestra playing, Symphony Center

6 **Chicago Temple**
MAP J4 ■ 77 W. Washington St.

A Gothic-inspired structure designed by Holabird and Roche in 1923. Under the majestic spire is a 35-seat chapel.

7 **Federal Reserve Bank**
MAP K4 ■ 230 S. LaSalle St.

This impressive edifice is one of 12 regional Reserve banks. When it was first built in 1922, it had the largest bank vaults ever constructed.

The logo of Chicago's Foodseum

8 **Foodseum Chicago**
MAP K3 ■ 19 N. Dearborn St.
■ www.foodseum.org

This museum presents rotating exhibits devoted to food, often with a local bent, such as hot dogs and Chicago's role in popularizing them.

9 **Palmer House Hilton**
The first Palmer House (see p117) was destroyed in the Great Chicago Fire (see p40). The current hotel is decorated with frescos, Tiffany light fixtures, and marble floors.

10 **Daley Plaza**
MAP K4

Home to the county court head-quarters, Daley Plaza is best known for its unnamed giant steel Picasso sculpture (1967) donated by the artist.

Shops

View from the upper floors, Macy's

1 Macy's
MAP K4 ■ 111 N. State St.

Once Marshall Field's, Chicago's oldest and best-known department store is famous for its elaborate Christmas displays, dazzling Tiffany dome, and iconic clock. Established more than 100 years ago, it offers top clothing and homeware (see p62).

2 TJ Maxx
MAP K4 ■ 11 N. State St.

This department store offers a wide variety of clothing for adults and children. A great place to find quality brands at the cheapest prices.

3 Block 37
MAP K4 ■ 108 N. State St.

The Loop's answer to the malls of The Magnificent Mile contains brands such as Sephora and Zara. Its food hall is great for lunch.

4 H&M
MAP K4 ■ 22 N. State St.

This bargain store offers trendy clothes for all occasions, including a collection especially suited for teenagers and under-30s.

5 Old Navy
MAP K4 ■ 150 N. State St.

This regional flagship store offers the ultimate Old Navy shopping experience, with two floors of discount jeans and T-shirts, and other casual comfort clothes.

6 Jewelers Center
MAP K4 ■ 5 S. Wabash Ave.
■ Closed Sun

On the strip commonly known as "Jewelers Row" this 1912 Art Deco building contains over 180 jewelers. It is a friendly place to shop for gold, pearls, watches, diamonds, and gems at relatively low prices.

7 Nordstrom Rack
MAP K4 ■ 24 N. State St.

High style on sale at a fraction of the original prices lures bargain hunters to this charming little sister of the upscale and pricey Nordstrom.

8 Blick Art Materials
MAP K4 ■ 42 S. State St.

This two-story family-owned store offers a wide range of cards, stationery and arty gifts in addition to its massive stock of fine art supplies.

9 Gallery 37 Store
MAP L4 ■ 66 E. Randolph St.

Teenage artists involved in an arts training program create the incredible paintings, sculptures, and other artworks sold here. All proceeds from sales are returned to the program.

10 Iwan Ries & Co.
MAP L4 ■ 19 S. Wabash Ave.
■ Closed Sun

Trading since 1857, this store sells a vast selection of cigars, pipes, and smoking accessories.

Places to Eat and Drink

PRICE CATEGORIES

Price categories include a three-course meal for one, a glass of house wine, tax, and a 15–20 percent tip.

$ under $30 $$ $30–$60 $$$ over $60

1 Everest
MAP K5 ■ 440 S. LaSalle St.
■ 312-663-8920 ■ Closed lunch, Sun & Mon ■ $$$

The restaurant on the top floor of the Chicago Stock Exchange has spectacular views and chocolate soufflé to die for.

2 The Gage
MAP L4 ■ 24 S. Michigan Ave.
■ 312-372-4243 ■ $$

Across from Millennium Park, this popular restaurant occupies a series of 19th-century millinery shops and has a vaguely Irish concept, serving Guinness on draft. The extensive menu highlights contemporary seasonal dishes.

3 Pizzeria Uno
MAP L3 ■ 29 E. Ohio St.
■ 312-321-1000 ■ $

Famous for its gooey deep-dish pizza, this spot (see p60) is a must-visit for anyone in search of true Chicago-style pizza.

4 Girl & the Goat
MAP H4 ■ 809 W. Randolph St.
■ 312-492-6262 ■ $$$

Top Chef winner Stephanie Izard runs this famous restaurant (see p60) serving goat and other bold-flavored dishes. Reservations or early arrivals are a must.

5 Lou Mitchell's
MAP J4 ■ 565 W. Jackson Blvd.
■ 312-939-3111 ■ No credit cards
■ No dinner ■ $

Head to Lou's (see p60) for a classic diner breakfast including to-die-for homemade skillet hashbrowns and double-yolk eggs. Expect a queue, though it'll move quickly.

6 Petterino's
MAP K4 ■ 150 Dearborn St.
■ 312-422-0150 ■ $$

This restaurant looks like a supper club with its jacketed waiters, but it operates with modern efficiency. Good pastas and chops are on the menu, and the bar is a popular post-curtain haunt for actors.

7 Atwood Café
MAP K4 ■ The Alise Chicago, 1 W. Washington St. ■ 312-368-1900 ■ $$

Expect top-notch hotel dining, where creative American cuisine leans toward comfort food.

Chic decor and great views at Cindy's

8 Cindy's
MAP L4 ■ 12 S. Michigan Ave.
■ 312-792-3502 ■ $$$

Crowds flock to Cindy's for the views. Its menu caters to a convivial crowd, with dishes such as seafood platters served at picnic-inspired tables.

9 Avec
MAP J4 ■ 615 W. Randolph St.
■ 312-377-2002 ■ Closed lunch, Mon ■ $$

Known for its cozy, wood-paneled dining room, Avec (see p61) serves shareable Mediterranean bites and wines that pair perfectly.

10 Terzo Piano
MAP L4 ■ 159 E. Monroe Dr.
■ 312-443-8650 ■ $$

Located on the third floor of the Art Institute, Terzo Piano serves superb Italian café fare by Michelin-starred chef Tony Mantuano.

See map on pp70–71

TOP 10 Near North

History, culture, and commerce collide on Chicago's densely packed Near North side. This area is a pleasure to explore on foot, whether you are interested in shopping or fine art and architecture. The city's classiest shopping boulevard – The Magnificent Mile – bridges the posh 19th-century mansions of the lakeside Gold Coast (which has its own clutch of upscale boutiques) and the former industrial warehouses of River North, now mostly converted into art galleries. In addition to these, there are two local art museums. But ultimately, it's The Magnificent Mile on a Saturday that says more about Midwestern vitality and giddy American consumerism than any other Chicago experience.

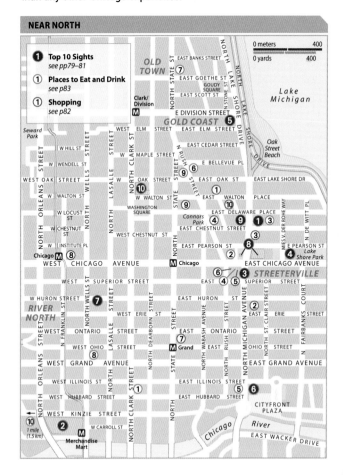

NEAR NORTH

1 **Top 10 Sights**
see pp79–81

1 **Places to Eat and Drink**
see p83

1 **Shopping**
see p82

1 John Hancock Center
MAP L2 ■ 875 N. Michigan
Ave. ■ Observatory: open 9am–11pm
daily; adm; www.360chicago.com
■ Signature Room and Lounge: open
daily; www.signatureroom.com

Skidmore, Owings & Merrill designed
this 1970 landmark using the signature Xs on the facade as cross-braces
to help the 1,100-ft (335-m) building
withstand the winds coming off Lake
Michigan. Soak up the view from the
94th-floor 360 Chicago, home to the
interactive TILT viewing experience,
or drink it in from the Signature
Room restaurant and lounge directly
above. Many say you get a better
view from here than from the South
Side's Sears Tower.

2 Merchandise Mart
MAP K3 ■ 222 W. Merchandise
Mart Plaza

This massive two-square-block
edifice houses Chicago's premier
interior design trade showrooms.
When completed in 1930, the four
million-sq-ft (390,000-sq-m) building
was the largest in the world. Today,
it is second only to the Pentagon in
size, and is one of the world's largest
commercial buildings. The Chicago
Architecture Center (see p31) offers
a 45-minute guided tour, which is a
great way to get to grips with this
daunting building.

Luxury stores at The Magnificent Mile

3 The Magnificent Mile
Whether you're a serial
shopper or not, this store-lined
strip (see pp32–3) warrants a visit
if only to get a feel for the commercial pulse that seems to keep
Chicago humming.

4 Museum of Contemporary Art
MAP L2 ■ 220 E. Chicago Ave.
■ Open 10am–9pm Tue, 10am–5pm
Wed–Sun ■ www.mcachicago.org

One of the country's largest
collections of contemporary art, the
MCA has over 6,000 objects, from
paintings and sculptures to photography and video installations. In
summer, the sculpture garden and
displays of performance art on the
front lawn enhance the experience.

The impressive stairwell, Museum of Contemporary Art

The historic Gold Coast Area

5 Gold Coast Area
MAP K1

Chicago has a number of upscale neighborhoods, but none more historic and prestigious than the Gold Coast. Railroad, retail, and lumber tycoons built this elegant district in the decades following the Great Fire of 1871 *(see p40)*, and its leafy streets are lined with 19th-century mansions interspersed with early 20th-century apartment buildings. There are no fewer than 300 designated historic landmarks in the Astor Street District alone, including buildings by Stanford White (such as 20 E. Burton Place), and Charnley House (1365 N. Astor Street), designed by Louis Sullivan (assisted at the time by Frank Lloyd Wright).

6 Tribune Tower
MAP L3 ■ 435 N Michigan Ave.

Topped by flying buttresses, this Gothic-style building was completed in 1925. Its faux-historic design had won a competition organized by Colonel Robert McCormick, publisher of the *Chicago Tribune*, the newspaper whose offices occupied the building until 2018. Look closely at the facade, which is embedded with over 120 stones collected by correspondents from famed sights. There's a rock hailing from each of the 50 states, as well as fragments from international monuments such as Greece's Parthenon, India's Taj Mahal, and The Great Wall of China.

7 River North Gallery District
MAP K3 ■ Bounded by Merchandise Mart (south), Chicago Ave. (north), Orleans Ave. (west), Dearborn St. (east) ■ Chicago Gallery News: 312-649-0064; www.chicagogallerynews.com

Said to be the most concentrated art hub in the US outside of Manhattan, this district is jammed with galleries. Most are found in the handsome, 19th-century converted brick warehouses found alongside the "L" brown line. Huron and Superior streets are particularly worth a visit.

8 Chicago Water Works and Pumping Station
MAP L2 ■ Water Works and Pumping Station: 163 E. Pearson St. & 806 N. Michigan Ave. ■ Visitor Center: 312-337-0665; open 7:30am–7pm Mon–Thu; www.choosechicago.com ■ City Gallery: 312-742-0808; open 10am–7pm Mon–Fri, 10am–5pm Sat & Sun

When the Great Fire of 1871 swept north, only the 1869 Water Works and Pumping Station escaped. Built by William W. Botington, the Gothic-Revival Water Works was modeled after a medieval castle. It now houses the Chicago Visitor Center and the Lookingglass Theatre *(see p55)*, and the fountain and chairs outside make it a focal point for street life. The functioning Pumping Station across the street houses the City Gallery, which specializes in photography.

Chicago Water Works

9 Fourth Presbyterian Church

MAP L2 ▪ 126 E. Chestnut St. ▪ Open 7:30am–9pm Mon–Fri, 7:30am–6pm Sat, 7:30am–6:30pm Sun

The first Fourth Presbyterian church, dedicated in 1871, celebrated its first sermon just hours before it was incinerated in the Great Fire. Rebuilt in 1914, the church offers a peaceful respite from The Magnificent Mile. Designed by Ralph Adams Cram, one of the architects behind New York's Cathedral of St. John the Divine, this church has a cathedral-like interior, with a splendid stained-glass west window. Free concerts take place on Fridays at noon.

Interior, Fourth Presbyterian Church

10 Newberry Library

MAP K2 ▪ 60 W. Walton St. ▪ 312-943-9090 ▪ Open 9am–5pm Mon–Fri (to 1pm Sat)

Founded in 1887 by wealthy Chicago businessman Walter L. Newberry, this research library is housed in a Romanesque-style granite building designed by architect Henry Ives Cob. It is stocked with rare books, maps, manuscripts, and music, and has research centers devoted to the history of cartography, American Indian and Indigenous studies, the Renaissance, and American history and culture. It also offers seminars on everything from Greek literature to genealogy research. The public can use the collections by applying for a reader's card, free of charge.

A DAY IN THE NEAR NORTH

▶ MORNING

Line up early with the locals for a fortifying stack at **The Original Pancake House** (22 E. Bellevue Pl.). Afterward, stroll south on Rush Street to Oak Street. Take a left and walk the most exclusive shopping block in the city, where you can pop into stores such as Tory Burch, Loro Piano, and more. Once you hit Michigan Avenue, it's a short jaunt to the **John Hancock Center** (see p79) for superb views. Back on terra firma, cross the street to the **Chicago Water Works** for a look at a piece of Chicago's history. Lovers of modern art should cross Michigan again and head to the **Museum of Contemporary Art** (see p79).

AFTERNOON

Everyone will get what they want for lunch at **Foodlife** (see p33) on the second floor of the mall in **Water Tower Place** (see p32). You can shop the seven floors of Chicago's first ever vertical mall, and then shop some more – and sightsee – along **The Magnificent Mile** (see p77). If you've worked up an appetite, stroll over to **The Drake** hotel (see p117) for high tea, which is served until 5pm.

EVENING

Catch a show at the **Lookingglass Theatre**, housed in the Water Works Pumping Station. Then head to chic NoMI in the **Park Hyatt Chicago** (see p83) for dinner and drinks with panoramic views of the landmark Water Tower and downtown Chicago.

See map on p78 ←

Shopping

① Patagonia
MAP L2 ▪ 48 E. Walton St.
Gear up for adventures of any scale at this outdoors outfitter, known for cold weather staples such as fleece jumpers and down coats.

② Nike
MAP L2 ▪ 669 N. Michigan Ave.
The Chicago flagship of the iconic sports brand is a massive bi-level space with eye-catching displays of sports gear and athleisure clothing, rotating exhibitions, and, of course, sneakers for miles.

American
Girl Place

③ American Girl Place
MAP L2 ▪ Water Tower Place, 835 N. Michigan Ave.
▪ 1-877-247-5223
Parents of girls aged four to twelve make a beeline for this store, the only retail outlet of the American Girl line of dolls. A theater and a café supplement three floors devoted to dolls, books, and other accessories.

④ Ikram
MAP L2 ▪ 873 N. Rush St.
Launched by a former Ultimo buyer, Ikram features high-end women's fashion sold at top dollar. Chic wares and lines change seasonally, but shop assistance is uniformly personal.

⑤ Polo Ralph Lauren
MAP L2 ▪ 750 N. Michigan Ave.
This massive, four-storied shop is a den devoted to everything Ralph Lauren. With numerous pictures of horses and hounds throughout, it is the biggest Ralph Lauren store in the world. It warrants a visit even from those who aren't as dedicated to the brand.

⑥ Anthropologie
MAP K2 ▪ 111 E. Chicago Ave.
Alternative women's apparel and stylish housewares gathered from around the world sell briskly at this large, loft-like store.

⑦ P.O.S.H.
MAP K3 ▪ 613 N. State St.
Recalling the days of elegant steamships and grand hotels, this store uses old-fashioned suitcases and steamer trunks to lovingly display vintage china and silverware engraved with hotel and ship logos.

⑧ Paper Source
MAP J2 ▪ 232 W. Chicago Ave.
This arty River North shop is part art supply store, part stationer. The creative selection of cards and small gifts includes handmade stationery, cloth-covered sketchbooks, and novel desktop accessories.

⑨ Marc Jacobs
MAP L2 ▪ 11 E Walton St.
New York designer Marc Jacobs is known for his handbags, but this boutique has a little bit of everything.

⑩ Bloomingdale's
MAP L2 ▪ 900 N. Michigan Ave.
An outpost of New York's homegrown department store that features in-store designer boutiques and a well-stocked shoe department.

Multi-level Bloomingdale's

Places to Eat and Drink

PRICE CATEGORIES
Price categories include a three-course meal for one, a glass of house wine, tax, and a 15–20 percent tip.

$ under $30 $$ $30–$60 $$$ over $60

Chefs at work, Nico Osteria

1 **Frontera Grill**
MAP K3 ■ 445 N. Clark St.
■ 312-661-1434 ■ Closed Sun & Mon
■ $$

Chef Rick Bayless' regional Mexican cuisine warrants the two-margarita waits that inevitably face diners at Frontera Grill *(see p61)*.

2 **NoMI**
MAP L2 ■ 800 N. Michigan Ave.
■ 312-239-4030 ■ $$$

On the seventh floor of the Park Hyatt Chicago, overlooking the landmark Water Tower, NoMI is a refined restaurant with a menu spanning sushi and steak.

3 **Signature Lounge**
MAP L2
■ 875 N. Michigan Ave.
■ 312-787-9596 ■ $

Located on the 96th floor of the John Hancock Center, the Signature Lounge offers pricey cocktails and lofty views. No minors after 7pm.

GT Fish & Oyster

4 **RL**
MAP L2 ■ 115 E. Chicago Ave.
■ 312-475-1100 ■ $$

This in-store steakhouse and power-eatery is furnished in upper-crust style by the Ralph Lauren Home shop. The menu is inspired by classic American food.

5 **The Purple Pig**
MAP L3 ■ 444 N. Michigan Ave. ■ 312-464-1744 ■ $$

Equally suitable for both happy hour spreads and coursed meals, this cozy venue *(see p60)* has a knowledgeable staff and buzzes with the clinking of its loyal patrons' wine glasses.

6 **Nico Osteria**
MAP K1 ■ 1015 N. Rush St.
■ 312-994-7100 ■ $$

Run by famous chef Paul Kahan, this Italian seafood restaurant serves crudo and oysters at its raw bar.

7 **Food Gallery**
MAP L2 ■ 1301 N. State Pkwy.
■ 312-229-6740 ■ $$

A jazz trio, opulent decor, and a classic continental menu serve diners at this historic lounge, formerly known as the Pump Room.

8 **GT Fish & Oyster**
MAP K3 ■ 531 N. Wells St.
■ 312-929-3501 ■ $$

Serves elegant food and fixed-price offerings at lunch. The raw bar is worth a visit.

9 **Gibson's Steakhouse**
MAP L2 ■ 1028 N. Rush St.
■ 312-266-8999 ■ $$$

For a classic Chicago steakhouse experience, this *(see p61)* is a go-to for locals and visitors alike. Try it for a leisurely lunch, or a loud dinner.

10 **Next**
MAP H3 ■ 953 W. Fulton Market ■ 312-226-0858 ■ Closed Mon & Tue ■ $$$

With a themed menu that rotates quarterly, this fine dining restaurant *(see p61)* serves to impress. Book online in advance.

See map on p78

TOP 10 Northside

Encompassing parts of Old Town, Lincoln Park, Lakeview, and Wrigleyville, Chicago's Northside boasts upscale restaurants and chi-chi boutiques galore, as well as some of the city's best bars and one of its most progressive theater companies, Steppenwolf (see p88). Older buildings have been transformed into beautiful condominiums, while stylish new apartments are springing up on empty lots. In season, nearby Wrigley Field fans bolster the lively Wrigleyville atmosphere by swarming the surrounding streets and bars. The vibrant, LGBTQ+ hub of Northalsted is also in this area, while running along Northside's eastern border is the incredible lakefront.

Rainbow pillar in Northalsted

NORTHSIDE

❶	**Top 10 Sights** see pp87–9
①	**Restaurants** see p93
①	**Shops** see p90
①	**Neighborhood Bars** see p92
①	**LGBTQ+ Bars** see p91

Previous pages Tiffany Dome, Chicago Cultural Center

Chicago Cubs playing to a full house, Wrigley Field

1 Wrigley Field
MAP D1 ■ 1060 W. Addison St.
■ 1-773-404-2827 ■ Tours daily ■ Adm
■ www.cubs.com

Built in 1914, this is the USA's oldest National League baseball park. The home team, the Chicago Cubs, hadn't won a World Series championship since 1908 (before the field even existed), but that changed in 2016, breaking the fabled "Curse of the Billy Goat." In season (March–September), spending an afternoon cheering on the "Cubbies" in this marvelous stadium, with its ivy-clad walls, is a quintessential Chicago experience.

2 Chicago History Museum
MAP F4 ■ 1601 N. Clark St.
■ Open 9:30am–4:30pm Tue–Sat,
noon–5pm Sun ■ Adm

Focusing on Illinois and Chicago history since settler days, this museum was established in 1856 and is the city's oldest cultural institution. One of the society's first donors bequeathed his collection of Lincoln memorabilia. The ex-president's deathbed is one of the items displayed. Visitors can climb aboard the Pioneer locomotive, while events such as the World's Columbian Exposition and the Great Chicago Fire (see p40), are brought to life by photographs, decorative arts, and other exhibits. There is also a collection of costumes from the mid-18th century to the present, belonging to famous figures, from George Washington to Michael Jordan.

3 Northalsted
MAP E1–2 ■ N. Halsted St.
(& much of Broadway) from Belmont Ave. to Grace St., & Clark St. from Belmont to Addison Aves

Just 40 years ago, this area – officially East Lakeview – was largely rundown. Today, it's home to artisan retailers, cool galleries, and popular clubs. Although Northalsted (recently renamed from Boystown) has long been known as a gay-friendly neighborhood, efforts have been made to make the area even more inclusive of the other LGBTQ+ communities.

Peggy Notebaert Nature Museum

4 Peggy Notebaert Nature Museum
MAP F3 ■ 2430 N. Cannon Dr.
■ 1-773-755-5100 ■ Open 10am–4pm
Thu–Sat ■ Adm

This museum's sloping, beige exterior was inspired by the sand dunes that once occupied its site. Inside are many engrossing interactive exhibits, the highlight being the walk-through Butterfly Haven.

5 Armitage/Halsted Shopping District

MAP E4 ■ Armitage Ave. from Halsted St. to Racine Ave., & Halsted St. from Webster to Armitage Aves

This area of unique boutiques is a boon for fashionistas. Dozens of shops here sell everything from sophisticated evening wear to high-end accessories. Many of the stores occupy renovated Victorian town homes, which are set along pretty, tree-lined streets.

6 Lincoln Park Conservatory

MAP F3 ■ 2391 N. Stockton Dr. ■ Open 9am–5pm daily

Take a free trip to the tropics at this spacious conservatory, just next to Lincoln Park Zoo. Opened in 1893, the glass structure is a year-round, 80° F (40° C) sanctuary from Chicago's bustle, and offers a welcome respite from the city's long winters. Paths meander past lush palms, flourishing ferns, and exquisite 100-year-old orchids. Avoid the crowds by coming on a weekday when, unless a seasonal show is taking place, it's a quiet space, with trickling water as the only background sound.

7 Lincoln Park Zoo

MAP F3 ■ 2001 N. Clark St. ■ 312-742-2000 ■ Open grounds: 7am–6pm daily; buildings: summer & fall: 10am–5pm daily (to 7pm Sat, Sun & hols); winter: 10am–4:30pm daily ■ www.lpzoo.org

Established in 1868 with just a pair of swans, the beloved Lincoln Park Zoo has become an important part of the Northside community. Wildlife such as tropical birds, big cats, primates, and reptiles thrive here in enclosures that recreate the various species' natural habitats. The activity-oriented AT&T Endangered Species Carousel and Farm-in-the-Zoo are must-sees for children.

8 Steppenwolf Theatre Co.

MAP E4 ■ 1650 N. Halsted St. ■ 312-335-2650 ■ www.steppenwolf.org

Founded in 1974 in a church basement, this theater company grew quickly to include a corps of actors who would become famous on stage and screen, including John Malkovich and Gary Sinise. Now based in a modern complex with two full stages and a smaller Garage Theater, Steppenwolf has sent many hits to New York's Broadway over the years.

Lush gardens in front of Lincoln Park Conservatory

⑨ North Avenue Beach

MAP F4 ■ Lakeshore Dr. &
North Ave. ■ Open dawn to dusk
■ Lifeguards on duty from Memorial
Day–Labor Day

When summer graces Chicago with
its presence, locals of all ages and
nationalities converge on this short,
but inviting beach. Running along
its edge is the lakefront path, where
cyclists, in-line skaters, runners, and
walkers stream by. Confident folks
strut their stuff at the outdoor gym,
sand volleyball courts allow the ener-
getic to let off steam, and the rooftop
bar of the steamship-shaped beach
house is perfect for a drink while
watching the activity below.

Jogging, North Avenue Beach

⑩ Second City

MAP F4 ■ 1616 N. Wells St.
■ 312-337-3992 ■ www.secondcity.com

It's hard to overstate the influence
that Second City has had on comedy
in America since it opened it doors
at North Wells Street in 1959. The
home of improvisational comedy,
Second City has been the starting
point for an army of talent from
John Belushi and Bill Murray to
Tina Fey, Dan Aykroyd, and Stephen
Colbert, and entire cast of the popular
TV show *Saturday Night Live*. On two
stages at its headquarters in Old Town,
Second City offers full-length shows
(another venue, UP Comedy Club on
West North Avenue, is reserved for
stand-up comedy). Improv seating
is first come first served and tight,
which just makes the hilarity even
more contagious.

▶ MORNING

Fuel up for the day at one of
Lincoln Park's favorite breakfast
joints, **Frances'** *(2552 N. Clark St.)*,
where a wonderfully fluffy French
toast is served. Afterwards, take
a stroll east down Wrightwood
Avenue and keep walking until
you come to the **Lincoln Park
Zoo**, where you can ride on the
wild side on the African Safari
motion simulator. Then, meet
all the animals before heading
for a lunch with a view at **Café
Brauer** *(2021 N. Stockton Dr.)*,
built in 1908 by Prairie School
architect Dwight Perkins.

AFTERNOON

During warm weather, head to
the lakefront along Fullerton
Avenue where you can stroll, rent
bikes, sunbathe, or even brave
the chilly Lake Michigan waters.
In colder months, catch a bus
(nos. 22 or 151) and immerse
yourself in the **Chicago History
Museum** *(see p87)*, or take a five-
minute cab ride to **Armitage/
Halsted Shopping District** for
some classy retail therapy.

EVENING

This part of town has many good
eateries: hop the "L" four stops
or take a cab to **Mia Francesca**
(see p93), a lively Italian trattoria
where the pasta dishes are big
enough for two, and there's an
excellent wine list. Round off your
day with a visit to **Kingston Mines**
(see p56) – just a short cab-ride
away – to hear some of the city's
best blues musicians.

See map on p86

Shops

1 Architectural Artifacts
MAP B3 ■ 4325 N. Ravenswood Ave.
This huge warehouse stocks cast-offs from period homes, factories, and offices. Interesting pieces, from old wooden doors to models used to make rubber gloves, offer a down-the-rabbit-hole retail experience.

2 Paper Source
MAP D1 ■ 3543 N. Southport Ave.
Originally an artist's supply store, Paper Source now concentrates on stationery and paper goods, ranging from origami papers and individual handmade gift-wrap sheets to stylish notecards and greeting cards. A craft area hosts workshops in card making.

3 Lori's Shoes
MAP E4 ■ 824 W. Armitage Ave.
Devoted shoe hounds flock to this store for its hot styles and discounted prices. The floors and walls are stacked high with boxes for a handy self-serve and try-on access.

4 Art Effect
MAP E4 ■ 934 W. Armitage Ave.
An institution on trendy Armitage Avenue since 1984, this eclectic boutique offers a little bit of everything, from offbeat fashion, accessories and statement jewelry to retro toys for kids and unusual homewares.

A quirky item for sale at Art Effect

5 Beatnix
MAP E2 ■ 3400 N. Halsted St.
This store boasts the best supply of costumes and vintage gear in the city, including wigs, distinctive mod jewelry, and make-up.

6 Andersonville Galleria
MAP B3 ■ 5247 N. Clark St.
Artists, jewelers, fashion designers, knitters, and more maintain booths at Andersonville Galleria, a creative co-op. You could easily spend a few hours wandering around the three-story maze.

Unabridged Bookstore

7 Unabridged Bookstore
MAP E2 ■ 3521 N. Broadway
Known for its large LGBTQ+ section, this Northalsted bookstore (see p87) also stocks books of all types, particularly childrens' books and books written in Spanish.

8 Scout Chicago
MAP B3 ■ 5221 N. Clark St.
An antique shop with a funky flare for mid-century modern and industrial one-offs, Scout always stocks surprises such as old gym lockers, in cramped, but intriguing quarters.

9 Uncle Dan's
MAP D1 ■ 3551 N. Southport Ave.
An outdoors equipment store with urban style that offers everything from mummy bags and tents to street-smart parkas that won't make you look like the Michelin man. There's a great selection of backpacks, too.

10 Brimfield
MAP B3 ■ 5219 N. Clark St.
Another of Andersonville's stylish vintage shops, Brimfield specializes in woolly plaids, from throw blankets to upholstered armchairs. Retro decorative items make browsing fun.

LGBTQ+ Bars

1 Second Story Bar
MAP L3 ■ 150 E. Ohio St.
Serving stiff drinks, this intimate bar is a great evening escape. Its friendly atmosphere (and small size) encourages visitors to mix.

2 The Closet
MAP E2 ■ 3325 N. Broadway
This dance club attracts a mostly lesbian crowd, but gay men and straight couples also groove to R&B, rap, dance, and diva videos.

3 Roscoe's Tavern
MAP E2 ■ 3356 N. Halsted St.
A young, preppy set packs this neighborhood bar for its antique decor, cozy fireplace, cheesy dance tunes, and, in summer, beer garden.

4 Sidetrack
MAP E2 ■ 3349 N. Halsted St.
Featuring four rooms, this vast bar has more than two dozen video monitors that highlight a different theme (such as show tunes or 1980s music) every night.

5 Kit Kat Lounge & Supper Club
MAP E2 ■ 3700 N. Halsted St.
■ Open dinner daily, Sun brunch
Martinis come in 52 flavors at this chic spot, where drag queens show their lip-synching talent.

6 Big Chicks
MAP B3 ■ 5024 N. Sheridan Rd.
A local LGBTQ+ community favorite, and one of Chicago's most welcoming bars, Big Chick's hosts popular trivia nights and Bear Den nights.

7 Berlin
MAP E2 ■ 954 W. Belmont Ave.
This edgy and friendly club attracts people from all walks of life. After midnight, the dance floor hits its peak, rocking with a stellar sound system and light show.

8 Progress Bar
MAP E2 ■ 3359 N. Halsted St.
Sit back and sip on must-try martinis while people-watching Northalsted folks through wall-to-wall windows at this sleek bar.

9 Elixir
MAP E2 ■ 3452 N. Halsted St
This dark little cocktail den is a nice antidote to the louder options down the street.

10 Hydrate
MAP E2 ■ 3458 N. Halsted St.
Hydrate features a bar in front with roll-up garage-style doors, and a dance floor out back that cranks into the early hours. A drag queen show "Beautie and Beaus" takes place on Saturday nights.

Pink lighting sets the mood, Kit Kat Lounge & Supper Club

See map on p86

Neighborhood Bars

The popular Goose Island Brewhouse

1 Goose Island Brewhouse
MAP D4 ▪ 1800 N.
Clybourn Ave.
Chicago's original microbrewery is a local favorite, with a range of beer styles and a full menu. Brewery tours are offered on weekends.

2 Schubas Tavern and Tied House
MAP D1 ▪ 3159 N. Southport Ave.
Twenty-somethings dress down for beer, live music, and a hip, new restaurant that packs in crowds, especially on the patio during warm-weather weekends.

3 The Tin Lizzie
MAP E3 ▪ 2483 N. Clark St.
A sports bar-and-dance club, Tin Lizzie is packed wall-to-wall with twenty- to thirty-somethings most weekend nights, when DJs spin a variety of tunes.

4 Map Room
MAP B4 ▪ 1949 N. Hoyne St.
With an impressive menu of global beers, Map Room draws an eclectic crowd of locals and travelers to swap stories and peruse its stacks of old National Geographic magazines.

5 Village Tap
MAP D1 ▪ 2055 W. Roscoe St.
Popular for its seasonal back patio, this bar in laid-back Roscoe village offers a strong selection of tap beers and pub food.

6 GMan Tavern
MAP D1 ▪ 3740 N. Clark St.
A Wrigleyville stalwart, GMan is not a sports bar despite being in the home of the Chicago Cubs . It has a range of beers and a few pool tables.

7 Delilah's
MAP D2 ▪ 2771 N. Lincoln Ave.
Called one of "the great whiskey bars in the world" by Whiskey Magazine, Delilah's has been a neighborhood watering hole for years. It has some 400 types of whiskeys on offer, not to mention the many beers on tap.

8 Lincoln Square Taproom
MAP B3 ▪ 4721 N. Lincoln Ave.
In the historically German district of Lincoln Square, this spot channels old-world gemeuthlichkeit, or warmth, with flower-box-trimmed front windows, German beer on tap, and an Alpine mural behind the bar.

9 The Whistler
MAP B4 ▪ 2421 N.
Milwaukee Ave.
A low-key cocktail bar, The Whistler buzzes with DJ sets and live jazz during the week, and fun dance parties on weekends. The storefront features rotating art installations.

Outdoor seating, Murphy's Bleachers

10 Murphy's Bleachers
MAP E1 ▪ 3655 N. Sheffield Ave.
Located just beyond the Wrigley Field, Murphy's Bleachers is a long-standing tavern with a loyal following among Cubs fanatics as well as fair-weather drinkers.

Restaurants

PRICE CATEGORIES
Price categories include a three-course meal for one, a glass of house wine, tax, and a 15–20 percent tip.

$ under $30 $$ $30–$60 $$$ over $60

① Alinea
MAP E4 ▪ 1723 N. Halsted St. ▪ 312-867-0110 ▪ Closed lunch, Mon & Tue ▪ $$$

This high-end, fine-dining restaurant *(see p60)* serves delicious unique food pairings in a very stylish setting.

② Mia Francesca
MAP F4 ▪ 3311 N. Clark St. ▪ 1-773-281-3310 ▪ Open dinner daily, 10am–3pm Sat & Sun ▪ $$

The wait for the generous portions of flavorful pastas, seafood, and chicken at this lively eatery is worth it.

③ Geja's Café
MAP E4 ▪ 340 W. Armitage Ave. ▪ 1-773-281-9101 ▪ Closed lunch ▪ $$$

The ultimate fondue in a romantic setting. Choose cheese or hot oil, or just opt for the divine chocolate fondue.

④ Fish Bar
MAP E2 ▪ 2956 N. Sheffield ▪ 1-773-681-8177 ▪ Open 11:30am–10pm Sun–Thu (to midnight Fri & Sat) ▪ $

This small eatery serves the best fish in the city – everything from salmon, oysters, and tilapia to classic fish and chips.

⑤ Smoque
MAP A4 ▪ 3800 N. Pulaski Rd. ▪ 1-773-545-7427 ▪ Open 11am–9pm Tue–Sun ▪ $

Smoque lures serious meat lovers with its pair of smoker grills churning out BBQ ribs, brisket, and pulled pork in St. Louis and Memphis style.

⑥ Longman & Eagle
MAP B4 ▪ 2657 N. Kedzie Ave. ▪ 1-773-276-7110 ▪ Open from 9am daily ▪ $$

This trendy gastropub takes its farm-fresh fare seriously but has a casual atmosphere in the two packed rooms.

⑦ North Pond
MAP F3 ▪ 2610 N. Cannon Dr. ▪ 1-773-477-5845 ▪ Open Wed–Sun from 5:30pm, and Sun brunch ▪ $$$

This pond-side restaurant (a former skaters' "warming house") serves up American gourmet cuisine *(see p60)*.

North Pond's beautiful dining room

⑧ Lula Café
MAP B4 ▪ 2537 N. Kedzie Ave. ▪ 1-773-489-9554 ▪ Open 9am–2am Wed–Mon ▪ $$

An eclectic café in Logan Square, Lula champions local and organic ingredients in its farm-to-table meals, from morning through late night.

⑨ Ann Sather
MAP E2 ▪ 909 W. Belmont Ave. ▪ 1-773-348-2378 ▪ $

Known for its scrumptious breakfasts, this Swedish restaurant also serves lunchtime specialties.

⑩ Boka
MAP E4 ▪ 1729 N. Halsted St. ▪ 312-337-6070 ▪ Open from 5pm daily ▪ $$

Boka offers elegant, seasonally informed food in a series of rooms.

See map on p86 «

回 South Loop

Just south of the business-centric Loop, this sprawling area mixes multicultural enclaves such as Chinatown (founded in the 1870s by migrant transcontinental railroad workers) with upper crust addresses, built after the Great Chicago Fire of 1871. The region has many Chicago "must-sees," but the jewel in the crown is undisputedly the impressive Museum Campus: here, the Field Museum, John G. Shedd Aquarium, and Adler Planetarium celebrate the wonders of the earth, sea, and sky respectively, collectively drawing over four million visitors each year. The highway that once separated the Field from its neighbors has been replaced by an inviting green campus, where cyclists and skaters join museum-goers on the plant-bordered paths in fair weather.

Figurine, Field Museum

1 Field Museum

One of the three lakefront institutions to occupy the Museum Campus, the vast Field Museum (see pp18–19) boasts a collection of more than 20 million fascinating natural history and anthropological artifacts from around the world.

Upscale homes on Prairie Avenue

2 Prairie Avenue District

MAP C5 ■ For walking tours (Jul–Sep) call 312-326-1480 ■ Clarke House: 1827 S. Indiana Ave.; adm ■ Glessner House: 1800 S. Prairie Ave.; adm

Of the wealthy enclaves both north and south of the Chicago River that emerged following the Great Fire of

SOUTH LOOP

WEST CONGRESS PARKWAY
UIC-Halsted
WEST HARRISON STREET
LITTLE ITALY
University of Illinois at Chicago
WEST TAYLOR STREET
WEST ROOSEVELT ROAD
ASHLAND AVENUE
LOOMIS STREET
RACINE AVENUE
S. MORGAN STREET
Halsted
WEST 16TH STREET
WEST 18TH STREET
WEST 19TH STREET
PILSEN WEST CULLERTON ST
WEST
LOWER WEST SIDE
South Branch
Halsted

1 **Top 10 Sights**
see pp94–7

1 **Places to Eat**
see p99

1 **Bars and Clubs**
see p98

1871, Prairie Avenue was the most fashionable and ritziest. Only a few of the old mansions remain today, of which two are open to the public (tour only): the Romanesque-Revival Glessner House, built in 1887, and Chicago's oldest building, Clarke House, built in 1836.

③ Blues Heaven Foundation

MAP C5 ▪ 2120 S. Michigan Ave. ▪ For tours call 312-808-1286 ▪ By appt only ▪ Adm

Located in the former studios of Chess Records, where blues greats from Muddy Waters to Willie Dixon once recorded, Blues Heaven has records, photos, and stage costumes dedicated to Chicago's blues style and its performers. The former label's music plays on the PA. There are occasional live performances.

Wild Reef exhibit, Shedd Aquarium

④ John G. Shedd Aquarium

Nearly 32,000 saltwater and freshwater animals live here. The second of the three Museum Campus sights, the Shedd is also one of the oldest and most visited public aquariums in the world *(see pp28–9)*. Dive in to discover the many treasures of the aquatic world on show.

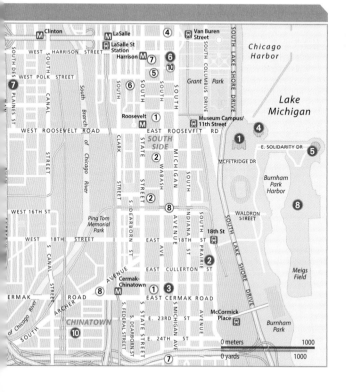

talks give curators and artists the chance to discuss the shows with museum-goers.

Star gazing, **Adler Planetarium**

5 Adler Planetarium

MAP M6 ■ 1300 S. Lake Shore Dr. ■ Open 9am–4pm daily; third Thu of month 6–10pm for "Adler After Dark" (over-21s only); for showtimes call 312-922-7827 ■ Adm

The first planetarium in the Western Hemisphere completes the Museum Campus trio. Visit its many galleries to walk among the stars, explore the worlds that orbit the Sun, and be enlightened by 1,000 years of astronomical discovery. Don't miss the Sky Theater show, which is projected on the 68-ft (21-m) dome of the historic Zeiss planetarium. The virtual reality events in the StarRider Theater launch you into the outer reaches of space and even give you the chance to interact with the show via a panel in the armrest.

6 Museum of Contemporary Photography

MAP L5 ■ 600 S. Michigan Ave. ■ Open 10am–5pm, Mon–Sat (to 8pm Thu), noon–5pm Sun ■ www.mocp.org

Run by and located in Columbia College Chicago, this museum is one of a kind in the Midwest. It exhibits the portfolios of international modern masters, with shows tending toward the experimental rather than the traditional documentary. Changing exhibitions also present a mixture of local talents and well-established ones, such as Gary Winogrand and William Eggleston. Frequent gallery

7 Maxwell Street Market

MAP J6 ■ 548 W. Roosevelt Rd. ■ Open 9am–3pm first and third Sun

Both 19th-century European immigrants and 20th-century African American settlers fleeing the Deep South got their entrepreneurial start selling from pushcarts around Maxwell Street. In 1994 the market was relocated to make way for the new University of Illinois at Chicago and, while a shadow of its former self, it still makes for a vibrant Sunday morning. Do expect plenty of Mexican housewares and used tools. The occasional treasure, such as a vintage fur coat, does show up, however. Another reason to visit is to try the homemade tacos from the Mexican food stalls that line the street.

8 Northerly Island

MAP M6 ■ 1521 S. Linn White Dr. ■ 312-745-2910 ■ Open 6am–11pm ■ www.chicagopark district.com

Northerly Island was part of city planner Daniel Burnham's plan for the lakefront to include a series of offshore islands acting as parks. At Northerly Island, Burnham's vision is now a reality. The green space extending south of the Adler Planetarium is the city's newest lakefront park, which hosts native gardens carved with walking trails, and an outdoor concert stage.

Lakefront strolling, Northerly Island

⑨ Jane Addams Hull-House

MAP H5 ▪ 800 S. Halsted St. ▪ 312-413-5353 ▪ Open 10am–4pm Tue–Fri, noon–4pm Sun ▪ www.hullhouse museum.org

When European immigrants were moving to Chicago to work in its rail and stock yards during the late 19th and early 20th centuries, Jane Addams bought Hull-House. From here, she offered social services and facilities to this immigrant working class, including day care, employment counselling, and art classes. Winner of the 1931 Nobel Peace Prize, Addams also championed the rights of women and helped usher in child labor laws. Her office, furnishings, and artwork are on display, and temporary exhibits tell the story of the settlement at Hull House and the invaluable work of its residents.

The famous Chinatown Gate

⑩ Chinatown

MAP B5 ▪ Around Wentworth Ave. & Cermak Rd.

Crowned by the landmark Chinatown Gate spanning Wentworth Avenue, Chicago's Chinatown isn't that large – running roughly eight blocks – but it is colorful. Home to Chicago's oldest Asian community, Chinatown was founded in the 19th century by trans-continental railroad workers fleeing West Coast prejudice. Cantonese and Mandarin are still spoken far more widely here than English. Stroll along Wentworth to admire the ornate On Leong Tong Building, buy fresh almond cookies from Chinese baker-ies, peruse the many import and herbal shops, or dine in one of the numerous local restaurants.

EXPLORING SOUTH LOOP

▶ MORNING

Start by grabbing coffee and an oreo cookie flapjack at **The Bongo Room** (1152 S. Wabash Ave., 312-291-0100). From there, walk through **Grant Park** (see p13) to Museum Campus. Here you can choose between the **Field Museum** (see p94), **Adler Planetarium**, and **John G. Shedd Aquarium** (see p95). If you plan to visit other museums on your trip, it makes sense to purchase a CityPass (see p65). If you opt to see the highlights of each, head to the Shedd Aquarium, where the Soundings restaurant offers good food and great views over-looking the lake.

AFTERNOON

Hail a cab (plenty wait outside the museums) or walk to the nearby pedestrian bridge at 18th Street to get to the **Prairie Avenue District** (see pp94–5), where you can stroll the historic streets and maybe even catch a tour of the **Glessner House** (see p95). Muster energy to catch a cab to the **Adler Planetarium** and walk south, enjoying the skyline views from **Northerly Island**.

EVENING

Head over to Wabash Avenue for an early supper at one of the trendy eateries on what is now a burgeoning strip. A popular spot is **Gioco** (see p99), known for its stellar Italian fare (reservations are recommended). After dinner, go on to **Buddy Guy's Legends** (see p98) and hear the blues.

See map on pp94–5 ←

Bars and Clubs

(1) Reggies
MAP K6 ▪ 2105 S. State St.
This rock venue and grill-pub offers nightly musical entertainment and good bar fare. Next door, Record Breakers sells rare vinyl and CDs.

(2) M Lounge
MAP K6 ▪ 1520 S. Wabash Ave.
Listen to traditional and modern jazz in style on comfy couches and low-slung seating in cranberry, chocolate, and sage. Stop by for live jazz on Wednesdays.

(3) Vintage Lounge
MAP G6 ▪ 1449 W. Taylor St.
The mahogany bar, classic cocktails, and chandeliers at Vintage Lounge will take you back to Old Chicago. A range of pizzas and homemade donuts are on the menu.

(4) Punch House
MAP B5 ▪ 1227 W. 18th St.
Hidden away in the basement of Dusek's restaurant, Punch House looks like a swinging 1970s recreation room. Potent punches are the specialty of the house.

(5) Buddy Guy's Legends
MAP L5 ▪ 700 S. Wabash Ave.
Run by bluesman Buddy Guy, this club is arguably the city's best. To get a table, come early and dine on decent barbecue food.

Buddy Guy's Legends

(6) Jazz Showcase
MAP K5 ▪ 806 S. Plymouth Ct.
Since 1947, this has been Chicago's premiere jazz showroom, hosting the greats past and present. Talkers will be shushed. Sunday afternoon shows are family friendly.

(7) Kasey's Tavern
MAP K5 ▪ 701 S. Dearborn Ave.
A local favorite, Kasey's has been serving Printer's Row regulars since the early 1970s — though the historic pub dates back to the early 20th century. In recent years, the beer list has grown impressively large.

(8) 16th Street Bar
MAP B5 ▪ 75 E. 16th St.
Craft coffee cocktails are a must-try at this friendly bar. It's popular with the nearby university crowd for both happy hour and date nights.

(9) Tufano's Vernon Park Tap
MAP H5 ▪ 1073 W. Vernon Park Pl. ▪ Closed Mon
Also known as Tufano's, this popular bar has legions of local and celebrity fans who pile in for some house wine and generous, inexpensive pastas.

(10) Hawkeye's Bar & Grill
MAP G6 ▪ 1458 W. Taylor St.
Try this sports bar for beer-fueled camaraderie and a genuine slice of Chicago fan zeal. A shuttle bus even delivers patrons to the United Center and US Cellular Field.

Places to Eat

PRICE CATEGORIES

Price categories include a three-course meal for one, a glass of house wine, tax, and a 15–20 percent tip.

$ under $30 $$ $30–$60 $$$ over $60

The informal Eleven City Diner

1 **Eleven City Diner**
MAP L6 ▪ 1112 S. Wabash Ave.
▪ 312-212-1112 ▪ $

Deli meets diner here, and breakfast is served all day. Come for sizeable sandwiches and old-fashioned fountain drinks, such as egg cream.

2 **Gioco**
MAP K6 ▪ 1312 S. Wabash Ave.
▪ 312-939-3870 ▪ Closed lunch Sat & Sun ▪ $$

Rustic Italian food is the draw at Gioco, a one-time speakeasy.

3 **Pompei Bakery**
MAP G6 ▪ 1531 W. Taylor St.
▪ 312-421-5179 ▪ No reservations ▪ $

This Little Italy lunch spot showcases a dozen delicious by-the-slice pizzas. Hot sandwiches and stuffed pastas round out the offerings.

4 **Cafécito**
MAP H6 ▪ 26 E. Ida B. Wells Dr.
▪ 312-922-2233 ▪ $

Cuban-style paninis, café con leche, and *batidos* (milkshakes) are the draw at this lively café.

5 **Davanti Enoteca**
MAP G6 ▪ 1359 W. Taylor St.
▪ 312-226-5550 ▪ Closed Mon–Thu ▪ $$

A charming wine bar and restaurant in Little Italy, Davanti Enoteca serves small plate starters, sharable larger plates including pastas and pizzas, and entrées such as grilled swordfish.

6 **Chez Joel**
MAP H6 ▪ 1119 W. Taylor St.
▪ 312-226-6479 ▪ Closed Mon & lunch Sun ▪ $$

A quaint French bistro in the heart of Little Italy charms fans with its sunny decor and fine classics.

7 **Moody Tongue**
MAP H6 ▪ 2515 S. Wabash Ave.
▪ 312-600-5111 ▪ $

A casual tasting room and a fine dining restaurant are housed under one roof here, with Michelin-starred chefs pairing bites with beer.

8 **Phoenix**
MAP A6 ▪ 2131 S. Archer Ave.
▪ 312-328-0848 ▪ $

Phoenix attracts dim sum diners from near and far. Go early on weekends or prepare for long waits.

Diners enjoying dim sum at Phoenix

9 **Rosebud Cafe**
MAP G6 ▪ 1500 W. Taylor St.
▪ 312-942-1117 ▪ $$

The Italian cooking at Rosebud's, located in Little Italy, isn't daring but its convivial vibe is hard to resist. Long waits for tables are common.

10 **Mercat a la Planxa**
MAP L5 ▪ 638 S. Michigan Ave.
▪ 312-765-0524 ▪ $$

Arguably the city's best Spanish restaurant, lively Mercat a la Planxa specializes in tapas such as bacon-wrapped dates and juicy lamb chops. Order suckling pig 72 hours ahead.

See map on pp94–5

TOP 10 Far South

Home to magnificent architecture, multicultural communities, and stand-out museums, such as the DuSable Museum of African American History and the Museum of Science and Industry, Chicago's Far South encompasses districts such as Hyde Park and Kenwood

that merit a journey off the beaten tourist path. Hyde Park and Kenwood began life as suburbs for the wealthy escaping the city; today, this part of town is incredibly varied and home to the University of Chicago students and to communities of Mexican, African American, Asian, and Indian heritages. Recreation and leisure options abound on spectacular tracts of green space, including the University of Chicago's Midway Plaisance and Jackson Park, site of the 1893 World's Columbian Exposition.

Detail of a relief, Oriental Institute

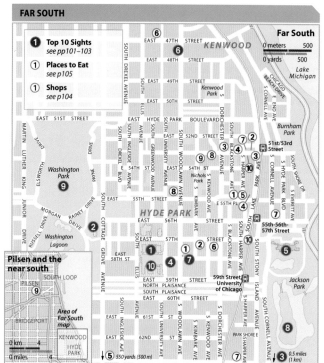

FAR SOUTH

1 **Top 10 Sights** see pp101–103

1 **Places to Eat** see p105

1 **Shops** see p104

University of Chicago campus

1 University of Chicago
MAP E6 ▪ 5801 S. Ellis Ave.
▪ Metra station: 55th St. ▪ 1-773-
702-1234 ▪ www.uchicago.edu
Noted for its research and high
educational standards, this remark-
able private university has produced
over 80 Nobel Prize winning alumni
and staff (see p50).

2 DuSable Museum of African American History
MAP D5 ▪ 740 E. 56th Pl. ▪ Open
11am–4pm Wed–Sun ▪ Adm (free
Sun) ▪ www.dusablemuseum.org
Located on the eastern edge of
Washington Park, this museum
is named after Chicago's first

Exhibits at the DuSable Museum

non-native settler, Jean Baptiste
Point du Sable. The permanent
exhibits celebrate other firsts, such
as the first Black US astronaut, Major
Robert Lawrence, and Chicago's first
African American mayor, Harold
Washington. Other thought-provoking
exhibits include rusted shackles and
the striking "Freedom Now" mural,
depicting 400 years of African
American history from the early days
of slavery to Civil Rights marches.

3 Stony Island Arts Bank
MAP F6 ▪ 6760 S. Stony Island
Ave. ▪ 312-857-5561 ▪ Open 11am–
6pm Tue–Sat
In 2015, contemporary artist Theaster
Gates, Jr., converted this once-grand
1893 bank into an exhibition and arts
space, fostering gentrification in a
region much in need of investment.
The center houses the record collection of the late Chicago DJ Frankie
Knuckles, considered the father of
House music, and over 60,000 glass
lantern slides from the art history
department at the University of
Chicago. Both collections can be
visited during free hour-long tours
offered every Saturday at 1pm.

4 Oriental Institute
MAP E6 ■ 1155 E. 58th St.
■ Open 11am–4pm Tue & Thu–Sun
■ www.oi.uchicago.edu

Learn about the origins of agriculture, the invention of writing, the birth of civilization, and the beginning of the study of arts, science, politics, and religion at this University of Chicago museum. Five galleries showcase ancient Near Eastern civilizations from about 3500 BC to AD 100; most exhibits were unearthed during the department's own excavations.

Museum of Science and Industry

5 Museum of Science and Industry
The largest science museum within a single building in the Western Hemisphere, this popular museum attracts over two million people a year *(see pp20–21)*.

6 Kenwood Historic District
MAP E5 ■ Boundaries: E. 43rd St. (north), E. 51st St. (south), S. Blackstone Ave. (east), and S. Drexel Blvd. (west)

This wealthy enclave within Kenwood was founded by John A. Kennicott in 1856. In the late 19th century this area was an upscale Chicago suburb, where wealthy residents built majestic homes on spacious lots, a rarity in the quickly booming city. A stroll around the district uncovers architectural styles ranging from Italianate and Colonial Revival to Prairie style, by influential figures such as Howard Van Doren Shaw and Frank Lloyd Wright *(see pp36–7)*.

7 Robie House
MAP E6 ■ 5757 S. Woodlawn Ave. ■ Tour times and prices vary; for information and to buy tickets, call 312-994-4000 or visit www. gowright.org

This splendid 1910 residence by Frank Lloyd Wright can be easily spotted by its steel-beam roof, which over-hangs the building by 20 ft (6 m) at each end. Take a tour through its low-ceilinged interior, past more than 170 art-glass windows and doors, to learn about the ten-year restoration program. The building was a private home until 1926, when it became a dormitory for the Chicago Theological Seminary. It was later bought by a development firm, who donated it to the University of Chicago in 1963, the same year it was designated a National Historic Landmark.

8 Osaka Japanese Gardens
MAP F6 ■ Jackson Park, 58th St. & Lake Shore Dr. ■ Open dawn–dusk

At the north end of Jackson Park's Wooded Island, lies this retreat, complete with meandering paths, lagoons, and fountains. The garden is a partial re-creation of the one formed in 1934 around the Japanese Pavilion built for the 1893 Expo, which burned down in 1946. The gardens were renamed in 1993 for one of Chicago's sister cities, Osaka, which donated the Japanese gate seen here.

Decorative bridges cross the lagoon, Osaka Japanese Gardens

9 Washington Park

MAP D5 ▪ Open dawn–11pm

Frederick Law Olmsted and Calvert Vaux, the designers of New York's Central Park, also created this sprawling green space in the early 1870s. It originally attracted mainly wealthy, city dwellers; but today, it is a widely used park with recreational programs, the DuSable Museum of African American History, and Lorado Taft's 110-ft (34-m) long sculpture, *Fountain of Time*, which took him 14 years to build.

Lorado Taft's sculpture, Washington Park

10 University of Chicago Sculptures

Over the years, the University of Chicago has acquired around 12 outdoor sculptures, including Wolf Vostell's playful 1970 *Concrete Traffic*, a car embedded in concrete at the southwest end of Midway Plaisance, and *Nuclear Energy*, a bronze sculpture by Henry Moore, that resembles a mushroom cloud. Within a reflecting pool at 60th Street and University Avenue is *Construction in Space in the Third and Fourth Dimension*, an abstract work created in the 1950s by Constructivist Antoine Pevsner. The striking piece depicts the space-time continuum.

EXPLORING FAR SOUTH

▶ MORNING

Start your day with a true South Side classic, the cafeteria **Valois** *(see p105)*, which draws everyone from local pensioners to former President Obama. From there, walk about a mile (1.6 km) south or hop on the no. 28 bus at the corner of Hyde Park Boulevard and Lake Park Avenue to visit the **Museum of Science and Industry**, where you can easily spend an engrossing few hours exploring the hands-on exhibits. For lunch, skip the museum food and head west about a mile (1.6 km) to **Medici on 57th** *(see p105)*, a great student and faculty hangout, known for its delicious pizzas. The extravagant Garbage Pizza is a favorite.

AFTERNOON

Stroll about four blocks southwest to the **Oriental Institute** at the **University of Chicago** *(see p101)* whose museum will transport you back to ancient times. Its Suq gift shop offers unique souvenirs, such as a replica of an ancient board game. Just east of the institute is Frank Lloyd Wright's masterpiece of Prairie-style architecture, **Robie House**. Take a tour of this to really gain some insight into the great man's vision. Then stroll around the university's leafy quadrangles, if weather permits, or backtrack a little to the **Smart Museum of Art** *(see p50)* if you'd rather be inside. Either way, round off your day with a delicious meal at **Plein Air Cafe** *(see p105)*, whose courtyard has views of Robie House.

See map on p100 ←

Shops

Shelves stacked high, Seminary Co-op Bookstore

1 Seminary Co-op Bookstore

MAP E6 ▪ 5751 S. Woodlawn Ave.

Housed in the basement of the Chicago Theological Seminary on the University of Chicago campus, this bookstore has a well-respected academic section, especially humanities and social sciences.

2 57th Street Books

MAP E6 ▪ 1301 E. 57th St.

This basement-level shop carries a range of new adult fiction, and children's books. Low ceilings, brick walls, and a painted cement floor all create a cozy atmosphere, conducive to browsing.

3 Hyde Park Records

MAP E5 ▪ 1377 E. 53rd St.

A favorite haunt of local musicians and a must-visit for touring DJs, Hyde Park Records specializes in vintage jazz, old soul, blues, gospel, and hip-hop records. Stop by its $1 sale on the first Saturday of every month.

4 Wesley's Shoe Corral

MAP F5 ▪ 1506 E. 55th St

Celebrating more than 50 years in business, Wesley's is the oldest continuously operating Black-owned shoe store in the country. Men's, women's, and children's styles are sold with friendly service.

5 Toys et Cetera

MAP F5 ▪ 5211 S. Harper Ave.

This inviting store focuses on good old-fashioned toys galore. Classic standbys include kites, face-painting kits, balls, and dress-up clothes.

6 Little Black Pearl Workshop

MAP C6 ▪ 1060 E. 47th St.

The gift shop at this cultural arts center sells the students' creations, such as one-of-a-kind painted furniture and vibrant mosaics.

7 Sarah Kuenyefu Collection

MAP F6 ▪ 1510 E. 63rd St.
▪ Closed Sun

The scent of sandlewood incense fills this small boutique that sells African artifacts, carved wooden sculptures, and albums of music from all over the continent.

8 Hyde Park Records

MAP E5 ▪ 1377 E. 53rd St.

This is the place to start up, or fill the gaps in, your record collection, with reasonable prices and friendly, knowledgable staff. New and used vinyl and CDs cover a wide range of genres, and there are some excellent bargains to be had.

9 Kilimanjaro International

MAP E5 ▪ 1305 E. 53rd St.

Reflecting the surrounding community's African roots, this fine arts and crafts specialty store features everything from hand-crafted jewelry to ceremonial masks.

10 Powell's Bookstore

MAP E6 ▪ 1501 E. 57th St.

Here, used books in top condition are stacked floor to ceiling on painted wood shelves, with antique editions protected behind glass.

Places to Eat

PRICE CATEGORIES
Price categories include a three-course
meal for one, a glass of house wine, tax,
and a 15–20 percent tip.

$ under $30 $$ $30–$60 $$$ over 60

1 La Petite Folie
MAP E5 ▪ 1504 E. 55th St.
▪ 1-773-493-1394 ▪ Closed Mon,
Sat & Sun lunch ▪ $$

An upscale French restaurant offering
a fixed-price menu, as well as entrées
featuring ingredients such as rabbit
and quail.

2 Valois
MAP F5 ▪ 1518 E. 53rd St.
▪ 1-773-667-0647 ▪ $

The cafeteria that proudly demands
that you "see your food," Valois offers
stick-to-your ribs comfort food, from
roast beef to goulash. Cash only.

3 The Promontory
MAP F5 ▪ 5311 S. Lake Park
Ave. ▪ 312-801-2100 ▪ Open
5:30am–10pm daily ▪ $$

With a menu spanning snacks and
mains, the savory Southern food has
a farm-to-table focus. There is live
and DJ-spun music on most nights.

Outside terrace, The Promontory

4 Plein Air Cafe
MAP E6 ▪ 5751 S. Woodlawn
Ave. ▪ 773-966-7531 ▪ $

A charming café serving excellent
coffee and European-influenced bites.

5 Harold's Chicken Shack
MAP C5 ▪ 2109 S. Wabash Ave.
▪ 312-326-5575 ▪ $

Enjoy fast soul food, including catfish
and fried chicken at this casual,
authentic café.

6 Medici on 57th
MAP E6 ▪ 1327 E. 57th St.
▪ 1-773-667-7394 ▪ $

Great pizzas draw the crowds, but
sandwiches on home-baked bread
and rich milkshakes are also offered.
Guests are welcome to bring their
own beer or wine to accompany
their meal.

7 Virtue
MAP F5 ▪ 1462 E. 53rd St.
▪ 773-947-8831

One of Hyde Park's few fine dining
destinations, Virtue draws patrons
from all over town, and beyond.
The chef-driven restaurant serves
sumptuous Southern fare paired
with wines and cocktails.

8 Woodlawn Tap
MAP E5 ▪ 1172 E. 55th St.
▪ 1-773-643-5516 ▪ $

A casual atmosphere, good food,
and cheap beer attract all types
to this bar, especially for the tasty
burgers and sandwiches.

9 Dusek's Board and Beer
MAP B5 ▪ 1227 W. 18th St.
▪ 312-526-3851 ▪ $$

In offbeat historic surroundings,
Dusek's serves an upscale menu
with tap beer pairings. Upstairs,
Thalia Hall stages concerts under
a separate admission.

10 Chant
MAP E5 ▪ 1509 E. 53rd St.
▪ 1-773-324-1999 ▪ $

With its funky vibe, unique cocktails,
and global fusion cuisine, Chant is
great at any time, but its Sunday
brunch with live music is particularly
good – and a real bargain.

See map on p100 ←

Streetsmart

The elevated "L" train threading its way through the skyscrapers

Getting Around

Arriving by Air

Most international and many domestic flights arrive at **O'Hare International Airport**, one of the world's busiest airports, located 20 miles (32 km) northwest of downtown Chicago. Serving most major airlines, including most international flights, this large and sprawling airport offers free transportation between its four terminals via the Airport Transport System (ATS) train.

The Chicago Transit Authority's Blue Line "L" train connects O'Hare to downtown; follow airport signs that say "Trains to City." Trips take about 50 minutes. Taxis are available from the lower arrivals level of each terminal. When the roads are clear, it can take 40 minutes to reach downtown, but time can quickly double with traffic.

Car rental agencies are located near the baggage claim areas in terminals 1–3, and via courtesy telephones from terminal 5 (do not be confused by the numbering; there is no terminal 4 at O'Hare).

Midway International Airport is Chicago's second airport. Located 10 miles (16 km) southwest of downtown, it serves mostly domestic airlines, including several popular budget carriers such as Southwest Airlines. Taxis are available from the lower arrivals level; car rental agencies are located in the main terminal building; and

shuttle buses leave from right outside it. The CTA's Orange Line "L" connects Midway and downtown in trips of less than 30 minutes.

Available near baggage reclaim at both airports, **GO Airport Express** will drop off (and pick up) at any requested downtown location; book the return airport shuttle in advance. Several companies, including **Elite Chicago Limo**, offer private door-to-door services when booked in advance, at rates higher than taxis.

Regional Trains

Up to 56 **Amtrak** trains serve Union Station in downtown each day, ranging from cross-country routes to a commuter service to nearby Milwaukee. The nearest "L" stop to Union station is at Clinton, but it's a good walk, so it's often better to take a cab or bus to your destination.

Reservations are necessary on many Amtrack routes and advised for travel during peak periods: the summer months and major holidays. Seats can be reserved online or in-person. Fares vary considerably based on advance purchase, with the cheapest fares usually offered for tickets bought at least 90 days ahead of travel.

Although Union Station is just west of the Loop and close to downtown Chicago, it is not an easy walk to hotels or CTA trains when you are carrying luggage. If

arriving in Chicago by train, it is probably best to plan on taking a taxi to your hotel. You will find that taxis are plentiful around the station.

Local Trains

Short for elevated train, the "L" is nevertheless the name given to the entire Chicago Transit Authority (CTA) train network, including the sections that travel underground. The eight lines covering the city's central districts are identifiable by color: red, green, blue, brown, orange, pink, purple, and yellow. The red and blue lines run 24 hours a day (less often off-peak).

Train directions are indicated by the last stop on the line in the direction of travel. Trains arrive every 5 to 20 minutes, and the service is fast and economical. CTA's smart-phone app provides real-time schedules. The regular "L" fare is $2.50.

Metra, the commuter rail system, connects the suburbs with the city center. The 495-mile (795-km) system has 230 stations in the Illinois counties of Cook, Du Page, Lake, Will, McHenry, and Kane. It also services some cities in Indiana and Wisconsin. Downtown stops are Union Station, LaSalle Street Station, Ogilvie Transportation Center, and Randolph Street Station.

Metra fares vary according to the journey's length. Trains run frequently during rush hour and every 1–3 hours at other times.

Long-Distance Bus Travel

The main terminal in Chicago for **Greyhound** Bus Line is a few blocks from Union Station. It is not within easy walking distance to hotels in the Loop, so plan on taking a taxi here.

Although walk-up ticket sales are readily available, Greyhound offers substantial discounts for purchasing tickets online and in advance.

Megabus drops Chicago arrivals directly opposite Union Station and offers cheap regional transport between cities. Tickets must be booked online and are not sold by the driver or on the bus.

Public Transportation

The Chicago Transit Authority (CTA) – which runs Chicago's elevated train as well as the city bus network – is Chicago's main public transport authority. Security and hygiene measures, timetables, ticket information, and transport maps can be obtained from the customer service office or the CTA website.

Buses and trains are busiest during rush hours: weekdays 7–9am and 3–7pm. If possible, you may want to avoid traveling at these times.

Tickets

Ventra is the fare payement system used on all CTA buses and trains, Metra trains, and Pace buses. Disposable tickets and top-up cards can be purchased from ticket vending machines in "L" stations and select retailers around town (a list of these can be found on Ventra's website).

Disposable tickets, with a pre-set value covering a single ride or a day's travel, are best for visitors planning a short stay in the city, while the top-up card is recommended if you plan on staying in Chicago for a while.

Ventra's top-up cards cost $5, but the fee is waived if you order the card online or refunded if you buy in person and register online within 90 days. Preload the card with credit, then use it each time you travel; the relevant fare will be deducted as required. Funds can be topped-up at ticket vending machines or by using the Ventra app.

Unlimited-ride passes for more than a day's travel can also be added to Ventra cards.

Buses

The CTA bus network covers the entire city and the suburbs, and is especially useful for reaching the lakefront, which is not served by the "L." Keep an eye out for the blue and white bus stop signs.

Most buses run every 10–20 minutes from dawn to late evening daily. Night buses (indicated with an owl on the bus stop sign) run every 30 minutes 1am–4am daily. To board a bus, hail the driver and remain on the curb until the bus has come to a complete stop. All CTA buses are fully wheelchair accessible, with lifts and ramps available to use. Bike racks are located on the front of all CTA buses; most standard bikes will fit.

PACE buses also ply the city suburbs and are numbered 208 and higher. Most buses run daily, seven days a week. The PACE website features a useful live bus tracker, as well as timetables and bus route maps.

DIRECTORY

ARRIVING BY AIR
Elite Chicago Limo
w elitechicagolimo.com

GO Airport Express
w airportexpress.com

Midway International Airport
w flychicago.com/midway

O'Hare International Airport
w flychicago.com/ohare

REGIONAL TRAINS
Amtrak
w amtrak.com

LOCAL TRAINS
CTA
w transitchicago.com

Metra
w metrarail.com

LONG-DISTANCE BUS TRAVEL
Greyhound
w greyhound.com

Megabus
w megabus.com

TICKETS
Ventra
w ventrachicago.com

BUSES
PACE
w pacebus.com

Driving to Chicago

Those arriving by car generally do so via the busy Interstate highways, including I-55 from the southwest, I-57 from the south, I-88 from the west, I-90 from the east and northwest, and I-94 from the east and north. Route 66 from Santa Monica, CA joins I-55 before hitting the busy central streets of downtown Chicago.

Car Rental

Rental car companies are located at airports, major stations, and other locations in the city. All major rental car companies including **Alamo, Avis, Budget,** and **Hertz** are represented at O'Hare and Midway airports.

Most companies will only rent cars to drivers 25 years and older in the US. A valid driving license and clean record are essential. All agencies require a major credit card. Damage and liability insurance is recommended just in case something unexpected should happen. It is advisable to always return the car with a full tank of gas; otherwise you will be required to pay an inflated fuel price.

Be sure to check for any pre-existing damage to the car and note this on your contract before you leave the rental lot.

A useful alternative to renting a vehicle is the car-share service **Zipcar,** which offers rentals by the hour or by the day. Members should apply online prior to reserving

a car; charges include gas and insurance.

Driving in Chicago

Driving in the city is not recommended for visitors. Parking can sometimes be difficult to find and is often expensive in the city center; plus, heavy traffic is common. Those travelling to Chicago by car are advised to leave their vehicle in a parking lot and use public transportation or taxis to get around.

Rules of the Road

The **Illinois Department of Transportation** website provides information on road closures and weather conditions; it also features links to live traffic-incident maps.

Vehicles are driven on the right-hand side of the road in the US, except on one-way streets. The Illinois speed limit is 30 mph (48 km/h) on city and residential roads. The speed limit for vehicles on Illinois' open highways is 65 mph (105 km/h) and 55 mph (88 km/h) on metro highways. A minimum speed regulation in Illinois means you could also be ticketed for driving too slowly.

You must wear a seatbelt, and it is illegal to talk on your mobile while driving. A right turn on a red light is permitted unless a sign prohibits it. Left turns are not allowed at some intersections during peak times, or are allowed only when the green arrow signal is illuminated.

Roadside tests and fines for drink driving

are common in Illinois. If you suffer a breakdown, call the American Automobile Association **(AAA)** for help.

Parking

Street parking in Chicago falls into three categories: free, metered, and restricted. Downtown, free street parking is scarce. Metered parking is the most readily available option.

Parking garages and lots in downtown Chicago are common but can be expensive. Outside of the central downtown area, lots and garages are cheaper but harder to come by. Most are located around popular attractions like sports arenas and shopping districts.

In winter months, be careful not to park in snow emergency routes as your car may be towed.

Taxis

It is usually easy to hail a cab downtown and in popular neighborhoods in commercial areas; in residential districts, it's better to call for one. There's an initial charge, then a fee per mile and per extra passenger. A 10–15 percent tip is expected. Companies include: **Checker Taxi Assoc., Flash Cab Co.,** and **Yellow Cab Co.** The ubiquitous ride-sharing service Uber also operates in the city.

May through September, **Chicago Water Taxi** runs boats between the Wrigley Building and a stop for both Union Station and the Ogilvie Transportation Center. **Shoreline Water**

Taxis also offers a frequent service on the Chicago River to Willis Tower, as well as to popular attractions on Lake Michigan, such as Navy Pier and the John G. Shedd Aquarium.

Guided Tours

Excellent walking, coach, and boat tours are offered by the Chicago Architecture Center (**CAC**). A fabulous way to get away from the tourist center and discover a few of Chicago's 77 neighborhoods is to take one of the Saturday tours with **Chicago Neighborhood Tours**. **Chicago Trolley Company** sells an all-day hop-on hop-off pass for self-guided tours. **Chicago Detours** offers guided tours with iPads that include interior architecture and a historic pub crawl.

Boat tour season is from April to October. Several companies offer Lake Michigan and Chicago River excursions. Lake Michigan cruises depart regularly from Navy Pier, and river tours depart from the Michigan Avenue Bridge. Prices vary. Many companies offer discounts when two or more tours per person are purchased; be sure to ask.

Cycle Hire

Cycling is a popular form of transport in Chicago. There are more public bicycle racks in Chicago than other city in the US, and more than 200 miles (322 km) of bike lanes on the city streets – most major throughways have designated bike lanes. However, cyclists on the streets must still use extreme caution, obey traffic laws, and wear a safety helmet.

The lakefront offers 18 miles (29 km) of scenic paths, although it can be busy. Informal rules of the road exist, but it is often difficult for walkers, cyclists, and in-line skaters to co-exist. The best time to enjoy the path is during business hours when traffic is quieter.

The city encourages short commutes via bicycle with its bike-share service, **Divvy**. Riders can purchase a 24-hour pass for $15 at any of the hundreds of Divvy bike stations around the lakefront bike paths.

Walking

The best way to explore Chicago, particularly downtown and Northside areas (including The Magnificent Mile and Lincoln Park), is by walking. Many of these central sights are within easy walking distance of each other.

Shopping areas are only a short walk from each other and streets are relatively flat, so you won't have to tackle many hills when out and about.

As Chicago drivers can sometimes be quite aggressive, pedestrians should never solely rely on the traffic lights; look both ways before crossing the street, and watch out for cars making right turns or racing through yellow lights.

During rush hour, traffic is sometimes controlled by traffic police.

DIRECTORY

CAR RENTAL
Alamo
🌐 goalamo.com
Avis
🌐 avis.com
Budget
🌐 budget.com
Hertz
🌐 hertz.com
Zipcar
🌐 zipcar.com

RULES OF THE ROAD
AAA
📞 800 222 4357
🌐 aaa.com
Illinois Department of Transportation
🌐 idot.illinois.gov

TAXI
Checker Taxi Assoc.
🌐 checkertaxichicago.com
Chicago Water Taxi
🌐 chicagowatertaxi.com
Flash Cab Co.
🌐 flashcab.com
Shoreline Water Taxis
🌐 shorelinesightseeing.com
Yellow Cab Co.
🌐 yellowcabchicago.com

GUIDED TOURS
CAC
🌐 architecture.org
Chicago Detours
🌐 chicagodetours.com
Chicago Neighborhood Tours
🌐 chicagoneighborhoodtours.com
Chicago Trolley Company
🌐 chicagotrolley.com

CYCLE HIRE
Divvy
🌐 divvybikes.com

Practical Information

Passports and Visas

For entry requirements, including visas, consult your nearest US embassy or check the **US Department of State**. Citizens of EU countries, Australia, Chile, Iceland, New Zealand, Japan, and the UK can spend up to 90 days in the US without a visa, so long as they have a valid passport and a round-trip ticket. They will also need to register with the **US Department of Homeland Security** and pay a fee online, prior to departure. Canadian citizens must show a valid passport. Citizens of other countries should contact their local US embassy well in advance of their trip to obtain the relevant visa.

Government Advice

Now more than ever, it is important to consult both your and the US government's advice before traveling. The **UK Foreign and Commonwealth Office**, the **Australian Department of Foreign Affairs and Trade**, and the US Department of State offer the latest information on security, health and local regulations.

Customs Information

You can find information on the laws relating to goods and currency taken in and out of the US on the **US Customs and Border Protection Agency** website. Passengers may carry $100 in gifts; 1 liter of alcohol as beer, wine, or liquor (if aged 21 years or older); 200 cigarettes, 100 cigars (not Cuban) or two kilograms (4.4 lbs) of smoking tobacco into the US without incurring tax.

Insurance

We recommend that you take out a comprehensive insurance policy covering theft, loss of belongings, medical care, cancellations and delays, and read the small print carefully. Medical insurance is highly recommended for international travelers to the US, as costs for medical and dental care can be high. Car rental agencies offer vehicle and liability insurance, but check your policy before traveling.

Health

The US has a world-class healthcare system. There are plenty of hospitals and emergency rooms in Chicago. **Weiss Memorial Hospital** and **Northwestern Memorial Hospital** are close to downtown and the city's Northside, while **Bernard A. Mitchell Hospital**, at the University of Chicago, serves the South Side.

Even with medical insurance, you may have to pay for services and claim reimbursement after. Always contact your insurer before receiving any treatment.

Many dental clinics are open 24 hours and are available for emergency procedures. Check with the hotel concierge or contact the **Chicago Dental Society** for a referral.

Pharmacies are plentiful throughout the city. Many drug stores are open 24 hours. The most popular drug store chains, including **Walgreens** and **CVS**, all have pharmacies inside. The pharmacies in 24-hour drug stores are usually only open during regular business hours and often close on Sunday.

Chicago has extreme seasons. Visitors should be prepared for cold, windy, and generally snowy winters, and very high temperatures during the summer (see p114).

For information regarding COVID-19 vaccination requirements, consult government advice.

Unless otherwise stated, tap water in Chicago is safe to drink.

Smoking, Alcohol, and Drugs

The legal minimum age for drinking alcohol in the US is 21, and you will need photo ID as proof of age in order to purchase alcohol and be allowed into bars. It is illegal to drink alcohol in public parks or to carry an open container of alcohol in your car, and penalties for driving under the influence of alcohol are severe.

Smoking is prohibited in all public buildings, bars, restaurants, and stores. Cigarettes can be purchased by those over 18 years old; proof of age will be required.

Other than marijuana, which is legal in Illinois, possession of narcotics is prohibted and can result in a prison sentence.

ID

It is not compulsory to carry ID at all times in Chicago. If you are asked by police to show your ID, a photocopy of your passport photo page should suffice. You may be asked to present the original document within 12 or 24 hours.

Personal Security

Although much of Chicago is safe for visitors, there are areas, as in any city, that may not be especially tourist friendly, and things can change on a block by block basis. Use common sense and be alert of your surroundings and you should enjoy a stress free trip. As the most common crimes tourists encounter are pickpocketing and

purse snatching, consider leaving your valuables in a safe place at your hotel. Contact your embassy if you have your passport stolen, or in the event of a serious crime or accident.

The **Emergency Helpline** is for police, fire and medical emergencies. For non-emergency police matters, such as theft or vandalism, call the **City Helpline**.

Chicago has a long legacy of supporting the LGBTQ+ community. The first recognized gay rights organization in the US, the Society for Human Rights, was founded in Chicago and homosexuality was legalized in Illinois in 1962.

Women may receive unwanted attention, especially around the city's main tourist areas. If you do feel threatened, head straight for the nearest police station.

Travelers with Specific Requirements

The majority of restaurants, hotels, shops, malls, and museums are accessible to wheelchair users. Many sidewalks offer curb cuts that allow smooth passage when crossing the streets. Most buses and train stations are also wheelchair accessible.

The non-profit **Easy Access Chicago's** website has help for travelers with specific requirements. The **Mayor's Office for People with Disabilities** provides services to residents with disabilities and details on city facilities.

Museums and galleries such as the Art Institute of Chicago and the Museum of Science and Industry offer tours in American Sign Language and tactile tours for those who are visually impaired.

DIRECTORY

PASSPORTS AND VISAS
US Department of Homeland Security
🔳 esta.cbp.dhs.gov
US Department of State
🔳 travel.state.gov

GOVERNMENT ADVICE
Australian Department of Foreign Affairs and Trade
🔳 smartraveller.gov.au
UK Foreign and Commonwealth Office
🔳 gov.uk/foreign-travel-advice

CUSTOMS INFORMATION
US Customs and Border Protection Agency
🔳 cbp.gov

HEALTH
Bernard A. Mitchell Hospital
MAP E6 ▪ 5841 S. Maryland Ave.
🔳 773-702-1000
🔳 uchospitals.edu
Chicago Dental Society
🔳 312-836-7300
🔳 cds.org
CVS
🔳 cvs.com
Northwestern Memorial Hospital
MAP L2 ▪ 201 E. Huron St.
🔳 312-926-3627
🔳 nm.org
Walgreens
🔳 walgreens.com

Weiss Memorial Hospital
4646 N. Marine Dr.
🔳 773-878-8700
🔳 weisshospital.com

PERSONAL SECURITY
Medical, Police, Fire (all emergencies)
🔳 911
City Helpline
🔳 311

TRAVELERS WITH SPECIFIC REQUIREMENTS
Mayor's Office for People with Disabilities
🔳 cityofchicago.org
Easy Access Chicago
🔳 easyaccesschicago.org

Time Zone

Chicago operates on Central Time (6 hours behind GMT). Daylight savings time begins at 3am on the second Sunday in March, when the clocks are moved forward an hour, and are reverted to the standard time at 1am on the first Sunday of November, when they are moved back an hour.

Money

The US currency is the dollar ($), which is divided into 100 cents.

ATMs are the easiest way to get money. Most banks charge for ATM use and currency exchange.

Banks may offer better exchange rates than the exchange windows found at the airports, but rates vary and not all banks offer foreign exchanges.

Credit cards are widely accepted, even for small purchases. Some smaller establishments that only accept cash advertise this clearly on their windows.

Electrical Appliances

Electrical appliances in the US operate on 110–120 volts and use two-prong plugs. Non-US, single-voltage appliances need a transformer and an adapter, commonly available at airport shops, electrical stores, and large department stores.

Cell Phones and Wi-Fi

Many cafes and hotels offer free Wi-Fi, usually accessible by a password available on asking. The City of Chicago offers free public Wi-Fi in various hotspots around the city, including all 80 Chicago Public Library locations, the Cultural Center (see p71), Daley Plaza (see p75), and Millennium Park (see pp34–5).

Chicago has two area codes: 312 for downtown and the immediate vicinity, and 773 for the rest of the city, including the Northside and South Side. Dial 1 + the area code for any US number outside the code for the area you are in; you do not need to do this on a cell phone. To dial abroad, key in 011 + country code + city code (omitting any initial 0).

Most cell phones work in America if unlocked by your carrier. Check the costs and data packages available before you travel, or consider buying a local SIM card to avoid high roaming costs.

Postal Services

Most branches of the US Postal Service are open 9am–6pm Monday to Friday and 9am–1pm Saturday. Some neighbourhood locations may have more abbreviated hours, and others may also be open for a few hours on Sunday mornings. Many stores, including grocery and drug stores, sell stamps. The mailboxes are navy blue and are available on many street corners.

Weather

Chicago winters are usually intemperate, with frequent heavy snow and temperatures ranging from 13° F (-9° C) to 37° F (4° C). Summer days can be anything from balmy to boiling, averaging 69° F (22° C) to 84° F (30° C). Extreme weather conditions like winter blizzards, heavy spring rains, and summer heat waves are not uncommon, with springtime weather being particularly changeable. Despite the winds that can gust off Lake Michigan, Chicago's "Windy City" moniker is actually attributed to the verbose bid the city made in order to host the 1893 World's Columbian Exposition. The best time to visit Chicago is during spring or fall, when the climate is moderate. If you can bear the bitter cold of the festive season you'll see the city sparkle with Christmas lights – and you'll have fewer tourists to contend with.

Opening Hours

Office hours for businesses are generally 9am–5pm Monday to Friday. Shop and mall hours can vary but they are usually open 10am–9pm Monday to Saturday and noon–5pm Sunday. However, the Northside boutiques and stores along the Mag Mile often stay open until 7 or 8pm every evening, except on Sundays.

Banks are usually open during regular office hours only, which is normally 9am–5pm Monday to Friday, though most banks offer 24-hour access to ATM machines.

The city's museums and attractions keep their own hours, though many extend their hours during the summer season and some offer at least one evening with extended opening hours each week. It is always best to consult their websites before going so as to avoid any disappointment.

Most banks, shops, offices, and attractions are closed over public holidays including New Year's Day (Jan 1); Martin Luther King Day (3rd Mon in Jan); President's Day (3rd Mon in Feb); Casimir Pulaski Day (1st Mon in Mar); Memorial Day (last Mon in May); Juneteenth (June 19); Independence Day (July 4); Labor Day (1st Mon in Sep); Thanksgiving (4th Thu in Nov); and Christmas Day (Dec 25).

COVID-19 Increased rates of infection may result in temporary opening hours and/or closures. Always check ahead before visiting museums, attractions and hospitality venues.

Visitor's Information

Chicago has two main tourist information centers: located in the Chicago Cultural Center (see p71) and in Macy's department store (see p76) in the Loop. Opening hours are at least 10am–5pm Monday to Saturday and 11am–4pm Sunday (the Macy's location keeps department store hours). You can also get further information at the city's official tourism website **Choose Chicago**, which is updated regularly. For in-depth reviews of where to go and what to see, log

onto **Do312**, a detailed events and entertainment website. **Eater Chicago** offers comprehensive dining information. **Theatre in Chicago**, also online, offers up-to-date information on the shows around town.

For discounted admission to a number of worthwhile tours and sites (including some museums), the **Go Chicago Card** and the **Chicago City Pass** can be purchased. The Go Chicago Card provides access to 28 different tours and sites, and costs $85 (subject to change) for a 1-day pass and $175 for a 5-day pass (with reductions for children). The Chicago City Pass, which includes admission to five must-see sites, costs $110 ($90 for children) and is valid for nine days. Both cards can be bought at tourist centers as well as major must-see sites.

Taxes and Refunds

Chicago state and local sales taxes are among the highest in the country at 10.25 percent on all non-food items.

At most restaurants, tipping is expected for waiters at 15–20 percent of the bill before taxes. Taxes will add 10.7 percent to your food bill.

Accommodation

Chicago offers every kind of accommodation, from a berth on a boat to a luxury hotel. Most accommodations are in hotels, which vary from big convention-focused options to small and

stylish boutiques. The best in terms of location are downtown.

Hotel rates vary according to the hotel category, and the time of week and season. Peak rates are from April to December and often coincide with business travel traffic in town. This means weekends can be a good time to save, though summer rates are highest no matter what day of the week. Twin-bedded rooms are uncommon; most double rooms have either a queen- or king-sized bed or two double beds. Rates are subject to a 17.4 percent hotel tax.

The selection of B&Bs, listed at the Chicago Bed and Breakfast Association (CBBA), are a great way to see the city from a new perspective.

Places to Stay

PRICE CATEGORIES
For a standard, double room per night (with breakfast if included), taxes and extra charges.
....
$ under $200 $$ $200–$400 $$$ over $400

Luxury Hotels

The Gwen
MAP L3 ■ 521 N. Rush St. ■ 312-645-1500 ■ www.thegwenchicago.com ■ $$
Tucked discreetly above the Shops at North Bridge on The Magnificent Mile, the 300-room Gwen, lodged in the historic 1929 McGraw-Hill Building, takes its name from sculptress Gwen Lux whose relief panels adorn the hotel. Its fifth-floor terrace bar is a haven on the teeming street.

InterContinental Chicago
MAP L2 ■ 505 N. Michigan Ave. ■ 312-944-4100 ■ www.icchicago.com ■ $$
This former men's club (see p32) has stunning public rooms, including a swimming pool, and very comfortable guest rooms. The mix of historic charm with contemporary elegance makes it one of the city's most luxurious hotels

Sofitel Chicago Water Tower
MAP K2 ■ 20 E. Chestnut St. ■ 312-324-4000 ■ www.sofitel.com ■ $$
This striking, ultra-modern hotel features spectacular views, sumptuous feather beds, and marble bathrooms in every room. There is also a 24-hour fitness center.

Trump International Hotel & Tower
MAP K3 ■ 401 N. Wabash Ave. ■ 312-588-8000 ■ www.trumpchicagohotel.com ■ $$
Chicago's second-highest building (at 92 stories) houses this chic and state-of-the-art hotel. Stylish rooms have electronic amenities and floor-to-ceiling windows with views of Lake Michigan, the Chicago River, and the city skyline.

Four Seasons
MAP L2 ■ 120 E. Delaware Pl. ■ 312-280-8800 ■ www.fourseasons.com ■ $$$
One can expect the best at this grand hotel – possibly Chicago's most elegant. Lavish rooms command sweeping city and lake views, and the award-winning Seasons restaurant is a must-try.

Langham Chicago
MAP K3 ■ 330 N. Wabash Ave. ■ 312-923-9988 ■ www.langhamhotels.com ■ $$$
This luxury hotel bridges worldly splendor and mid-century modern Chicago, a cue it takes from its prime location in a Mies van der Rohe-designed high-rise. The popular second-story bar looks out over the Chicago River and the swanky Chuan Spa offers a wide range of unusual Asian treatments.

Park Hyatt Chicago
MAP L2 ■ 800 N. Michigan Ave. ■ 312-335-1234 ■ www.parkchicago.hyatt.com ■ $$$
Original contemporary art, rich woods, and warm tones create comfortable and tranquil public and private areas at this elegant boutique hotel. The state-of-the-art rooms and suites feature furniture designed by Mies van der Rohe. Other facilities include an indoor pool and fitness center.

Peninsula Chicago
MAP L2 ■ 108 E. Superior St. ■ 312-337-2888 ■ www.peninsula.com/chicago ■ $$$
Understated elegance sums up this hotel, with large, earth-toned rooms that include dressing areas, and a steam-free TV screen and hands-free telephone in every bathroom. Floor-to-ceiling windows dramatize the lobby, where afternoon tea is accompanied by live classical music.

Ritz-Carlton
MAP L2 ■ 160 E. Pearson St. ■ 312-266-1000 ■ www.fourseasons.com ■ $$$
The opulent Ritz-Carlton has it all – first-class service, an award-winning dining room, spa, and the best business facilities. Great views complement the classic furniture and fine art in its spacious guest rooms, but it's the little things, like Bulgari toiletries and toys and cookies for the children, that puts it in a league of its own.

Historic Hotels

Millennium Knickerbocker
MAP L2 ■ 163 E. Walton Pl. ■ 312-751-8100 ■ www.millennium hotels.com ■ $

This hotel, once owned by Playboy magazine, has hosted guests as famous as John Kennedy and Al Capone. Its 1930s lobby holds the Martini Bar (with live music most days), and the guest rooms exude a timeless elegance.

Palmer House Hilton
MAP L4 ■ 17 E. Monroe St. ■ 312-726-7500 ■ www. chicagohilton.com ■ $

This has been an elegant fixture in the heart of the Loop since 1873. Extravagant frescoes decorate the lobby's ceiling, while the guest rooms are subtly elegant. The hotel has its own shopping arcade.

The Tremont
MAP K2 ■ 100 E. Chestnut St. ■ 312-751-1900 ■ www.tremontchicago. com ■ $

An inviting fireplace welcomes you at this 1920s-built hotel, where guest rooms are small but comfortable; some have antique furniture and four-posters. Mike Ditka's restaurant is famous for its steaks and sports memorabilia.

The Whitehall
MAP L2 ■ 105 E. Delaware Pl. ■ 312-944-6300 ■ www.thewhitehall hotel.com ■ $

A quiet, understated European ambience has permeated this hotel since it opened in 1928. The 221 guest rooms combine elegant

tradition with mod cons, and the Presidential Suite was a favorite of Katharine Hepburn. Check out the Fornetto Mei restaurant with its menu of neo-Milanese cuisine and thin-crust specialty pizzas.

Chicago Athletic Association
MAP L4 ■ 12 S. Michigan Ave. ■ 312-940-3552 ■ www.chicagoathletic hotel.com ■ $

Originally opened in 1893 as a men's club, the reincarnation of this building as a hotel faithfully restored all the terrazzo floors, stained glass, marble staircases, and other adornments. The rooftop restaurant and the vintage-game-filled bar are among the highlights.

The Talbott
MAP K2 ■ 20 E. Delaware Pl. ■ 312-944-4970 ■ www.talbotthotel.com ■ $$

Enjoy the quiet elegance of this European-style hotel. The Victorian parlor-like lobby and atmospheric Basil's bar and café offer a chance to unwind. The 149 guest rooms and suites are large as well as welcoming.

Wheeler Mansion
2020 S. Calumet Ave. ■ 312-945-2020 ■ www. wheelermansion.com ■ $$

An immaculate 11-room hotel, this mansion dating to 1870 is known for its fantastic attention to detail. Marvel at the lavish artwork, period features, and antique furniture, or relax in the tranquil garden.

The Drake
MAP L2 ■ 140 E. Walton Pl. ■ 312-787-2200 ■ www.thedrakehotel. com ■ $$$

Popular with visiting celebrities and royalty, this is the grande dame of Chicago hotels. A landmark building on The Magnificent Mile, The Drake effortlessly blends modern convenience with the charm of days gone by. Each of the 535 rooms and suites is unique, and many of them offer breathtaking views.

The Alise Chicago
MAP K4 ■ 1 W. Washington St. ■ 312-782-1111 ■ www.staypineapple. com ■ $$

The Reliance Building (see p42) – an example of the Chicago school of architecture – was reborn as a boutique hotel in 1999 and has flourished since. Plush rooms are decorated in gold and blue, some with great views. Complimentary coffee and pineapple cupcakes are on offer every afternoon.

Designer Hotels

21C Museum Hotel Chicago
MAP L2 ■ 55 E. Ontario St. ■ 312-337-1000 ■ www.21Cmuseum hotels.com/chicago ■ $

Offering luxurious amenities without burning a hole in your pocket, the sleek 21C is a modern art museum and a hotel rolled into one. Rooms have comfortable platform beds, a small dining area, plasma TVs, stereos with MP3 docks, free Wi-Fi, and marble bathrooms. There's also a restaurant and spa on site.

Eurostars Magnificent Mile

MAP K2 ▪ 660 N. State St. ▪ 312-202-6000 ▪ www. eurostarsmagnificent mile.com ▪ $

Chic and contemporary, this boutique hotel has rooms with modern furnishings, floor-to-ceiling windows, Wi-Fi, a state-of-the-art sound system, fine linens, and a double-sized shower. Guests can enjoy a range of services available at the spa. The restaurant, Leviathan, serves delectable regional American dishes.

The Allegro Royal Sonesta

MAP J4 ▪ 171 W. Randolph St. ▪ 312-236-0123 ▪ www.sonesta.com ▪ $$

Designer Cheryl Rowley has combined classic Art Deco features with contemporary colors and textures to great effect at this vibrant, historic hotel. Complimentary wine is offered nightly to guests.

Godfrey Hotel Chicago

MAP K2 ▪ 127 W. Huron St. ▪ 312-649-2000 ▪ www.godfreyhotel chicago.com ▪ $$

Set in trendy River North, the Godfrey offers considerable social appeal via its rooftop lounge, partially glassed-in for four-season service, with a video wall and fire pit. Its 221 rooms are loft-like and amenities include a great spa and Italian restaurant.

Pendry Chicago

MAP L2 ▪ 230 N. Michigan Ave. ▪ 312-345-1000 ▪ www.pendry.com/ chicago ▪ $$

This extravagant 364-room hotel occupies the Carbide and Carbon building – an Art Deco creation of 1929. Stunning architectural details are everywhere, and the tower suites display artful luxury.

Radisson Blu Aqua Hotel Chicago

MAP L3 ▪ 221 N. Columbus Dr. ▪ 312-565-5258 ▪ www.radissonblu. com ▪ $$

In the undulating Aqua Tower, the 334-room Radisson Blu Aqua offers several amenities, including indoor and outdoor pools. The hotel's useful app offers a tour of its extensive art collection.

Soho House Chicago

MAP H4 ▪ 113 N. Green St. ▪ 312-521-8000 ▪ www.sohohouse chicago.com ▪ $$

Belonging to the stylish Soho House clubs, the Chicago branch occupies a 19th-century factory marrying refined and raw materials, such as exposed brick walls and chandeliers. Guests have access to a members-only rooftop bar and pool, private lounge, and gym.

Thompson Chicago

MAP K1 ▪ 21 E. Bellevue Pl. ▪ 312-266-2100 ▪ www.thompsonhotels. com ▪ $$

In a good location in the Gold Coast area, the 247-room Thompson Chicago features organic accents and intriguing art. Window-walled rooms, the higher the better, offer skyline views. One of Chicago's best chefs, Paul Kahan, runs the excellent Nico Osteria restaurant here, as well as the cocktail bar in the convivial lobby.

Virgin Hotels Chicago

MAP L3 ▪ 203 N. Wabash Ave. ▪ 312-940-4400 ▪ www.virginhotels.com ▪ $$

Sir Richard Branson has reinvented this hotel with good design and humor. Rooms feature sliding doors between the foyer and bedroom and ceramic dogs indicate pet-friendly rooms. Eat and drink in the first-floor diner or rooftop bar.

W Chicago Lakeshore

MAP M3 ▪ 644 N. Lake Shore Dr. ▪ 312-943-9200 ▪ www.wchicago-lake shore.com ▪ $$

A Zen water wall and "Leave me alone," rather than "Do not disturb" signs are indications of the W's hip take on the hotel experience.

Business Hotels

Courtyard by Marriott Chicago Downtown/ River North

MAP K3 ▪ 30 E. Hubbard St. ▪ 312-329-2500 ▪ www.courtyard.com ▪ $

Bright, modern rooms with high-speed Internet access, a spacious work area, and an extra sofa-bed make this centrally located hotel a popular choice among leisure and business travelers alike.

Hyatt Regency McCormick Place

MAP D5 ▪ 2233 S. Martin Luther King Jr. Dr. ▪ 312-567-1234 ▪ www. mccormickplace.hyatt. com ▪ $

Linked by a connecting walkway to McCormick Place convention center, the basic but modern rooms of the 32-story Hyatt Regency are an attractive stopover for conventioneers. The hotel also has a fitness facility.

Residence Inn Chicago Downtown/ Loop

MAP K4 ■ 11 S. LaSalle St. ■ 312-223-8500 ■ www. marriott.com ■ $

In a historic building in downtown the Loop, this extended-stay hotel offers more style than most in the category. Rooms are spacious and come with kitchens. There is a fitness center on site.

Embassy Suites Hotel O'Hare-Rosemont

5500 N. River Rd., Rosemont ■ 1-847-678-4000 ■ www.embassy ohare.com ■ $$

This hotel's seven-story garden atrium makes a pleasant retreat from the hustle and bustle. Suites have all the necessary facilities; cooked breakfasts and an airport shuttle are complimentary.

Hyatt Regency Chicago

MAP L3 ■ 151 E. Wacker Dr. ■ 312-565-1234 ■ www.chicagoregency. hyatt.com ■ $$

A lobby full of greenery and fountains welcomes guests into this large hotel. Although all guest rooms offer high-speed Internet access, you can opt for a "Business Plan" upgrade to obtain more specific benefits.

Sheraton Grand Chicago

301 E. North Water St. ■ 312-464-1000 ■ www. sheratonchicago.com ■ $$

The large, stylish guest rooms here offer fantastic lake, city, or river views.

The hotel has a business center, boat dock, health club, and five restaurants.

Swissôtel Chicago

MAP L3 ■ 323 E. Wacker Dr. ■ 312-565-0565 ■ www.swissotel.com ■ $$

Rising up where the Chicago River and Lake Michigan meet is this dramatic glass-and-steel creation. Oversized rooms contain every convenience for the business traveler and provide stellar views across the city skyline.

Westin Chicago River North

MAP K3 ■ 320 N. Dearborn St. ■ 312-744-1900 ■ www.westin chicago.com ■ $$

This sleek, four-star venue is home to a state-of-the-art Executive Business Center, fitness facility, and guest rooms featuring the comfortable Westin Heavenly Bed.

Budget Accommodation

AC Hotel Chicago Downtown

MAP L2 ■ 630 N. Rush St. ■ 312-981-6600 ■ www. marriott.com ■ $

Neutral rooms are calm, cool, and refined in this Gold Coast hotel. The lounge offers a pleasant space to start or end your evening, the restaurant serves breakfast only, and the fitness facilities include an indoor pool.

Best Western River North

MAP K3 ■ 125 W. Ohio St. ■ 312-467-0800 or 1-800-727-0800 ■ www.river northhotel.com ■ $

The location of this hotel, a little west of

The Magnificent Mile, is excellent. Rooms are spacious, with free high-speed Internet access, in-room movies, and 30 minutes of local calls. There are also parking, fitness rooms, and an indoor pool.

Freehand Chicago

MAP L3 ■ 19 E Ohio St. ■ 312-940-3699 ■ www. thefreehand.com ■ $

The stylish Freehand bills itself as a hostel, and offers shared rooms, but it also acts as a budget hotel and has small private rooms with their own bathrooms. Furthermore, its chic cocktail lounge and restaurant attract locals as well as travelers.

Hampton Inn Chicago Downtown

MAP K3 ■ 33 W. Illinois St. ■ 312-832-0330 ■ www. hamptonsuiteschicago. com ■ $

Located in River North, the Hampton Inn offers good value just a block from The Magnificent Mile. Amenities include an indoor pool, fitness center, outdoor patio, free breakfast, and complimentary Wi-Fi. The on-site restaurant Joe Fish features Italian food.

Hostelling International Chicago

MAP L5 ■ 24 E. Ida B. Wells Dr. ■ 312-360-0300 ■ www.hichicago.org ■ $

This place has a great value if you don't mind sleeping in a basic dormitory with local students. You don't need to be a member in order to stay here. The facilities include lounges, fully equipped kitchens, and bed linen.

General Index

Page numbers in **bold** refer to main entries.

Acknowledgments

Authors

Chicago-based freelancer Elaine Glusac specializes in travel writing for an array of publications including *National Geographic Traveler* and the *International Herald Tribune*.

Elisa Kronish ia a Chicago native who has written about the city's highlights and hidden finds for a varity of print and online travel guides such as Citysearch Chicago.

Roberta Sotonoff is a travel junkie. She writes about a variety of travel destinations, and her work has appeared worldwide in more than 40 newspapers, magazines, online sites, and guidebooks.

Publishing Director Georgina Dee

Publisher Vivien Antwi

Design Director Phil Ormerod

Editorial Michelle Crane, Rachel Fox, Sally Schafer, Jackie Staddon, Sophie Wright

Cover Design Bess Daly, Maxine Pedliham

Design Tessa Bindloss, Richard Czapnik, Stuti Tiwari Bhatia

Commissioned Photography Alessandra Santarelli and Joeff Davis, Andrew Leyerle, Rough Guides/Greg Roden, Jim Warych

Picture Research Susie Peachey, Ellen Root, Lucy Sienkowska, Oran Tarjan

Cartography Subhashree Bharti, Suresh Kumar, James Macdonald, Alok Pathak

Senior Production Editor Jason Little

Production Olivia Jeffries

Factchecker Lauren Viera

Proofreader Susanne Hillen

Indexer Rohan Bolton

Illustrator Lee Redmond

First edition created by Departure Lounge, London

Revisions Team
Meghna, Hansa Babra, Dipika Dasgupta, Shikha Kulkarni, Arushi Mathur, George Nimmo, Vagisha Pushp, Lucy Sara-Kelly, Beverly Smart, Azeem Siddiqui, Rada Radojicic, Akshay Rana, Priyanka Thakur, Vaishali Vashisht, Tanveer Zaidi

Picture Credits

Penguin
Random
House

13br; Grzegorz Kieca 72bl; James Kirkikis 71tr; Jessica Kirsh 73cl; Jesse Kraft 3tr, 106-7; Lightpainter 87t; Maisna 65cl; Marchello74 4t; Antwon Mcmullen 7cr; Mramos7637 32bl; Glenn Nagel 51cr, 62cl; Rhbabiak13 4cla; Michael Rosebrock 6cla; Rudi1976 10cl; Saletomic 11crb; Mario Savoia 72cl; Tehnik83 12bl; Theresasc75 11cra, 96br; Vplut 35tl; Wirestock 79b; Zachary Zuchowski 16b.

Courtesy of the DuSable Museum of African-American History: Dorling Kinderlsey Ltd/Santarelli Alessandra and Joeff Davis 45t.

Edible Ink PR: Stronghold Photography/Neil John Burger 91b.

Field Museum: 18cl, 19cb; Greg Neise 10crb, 19tr, 19br.

Foodseum: 75cr.

Getty Images: Timothy Hiatt 64tl; Bruce Leighty 94clb; Museum of Science and Industry Chicago 23tl; Scott Olson 63br; Helen H. Richardson 92tl; UniversalImagesGroup 43tl; The Washington Post/Brett T. Roseman 90tr.

Hogsalt Hospitality: California Clipper 57br.

iStockphoto.com: Kevin LEBRE 80tl; LevKPhoto 1; Sean Pavone 30-31c; stevegeer 24-5.

John G. Shedd Aquarium: Brenna Hernandez 53b.

Museum of Science and Industry, Chicago, Il: 20-1, 21cr, 22tl, 53tr; J.B. Spector 20cl, 20bl, 21tl.

North Pond Restaurant: 93cr.

One Off Hospitality Group, LTD: Jetel Fogelson 83tr.

The Promontory: 105r, Clayton Hauck 105clb.

Rex by Shutterstock: Courtesy Everett Collection 43br; KPA/Zuma 41bl; Paramount/Everett 49b.

Robert Harding Picture Library: Amanda Hall 79tr, 89cl; Henryk Sadura 48clb; Michael Weber 28-9.

Rosa's Lounge: 56tl.

Seminary Co-op Bookstore: Hedrich Blessing/Steve Hall 104t.

Shutterstock: James Kirkikis 92crb.

Thomas Hart Shelby- Goat Rodeo Productions: 77cra.

Ukrainian Institute of Modern Art: 45c.

Willis Tower/FleishmanHillard: 7tl, 71br.

Cover

Front and spine: **iStockphoto.com:** LevKPhoto.
Back: **Alamy Stock Photo:** Aurora Photos tl;
Dreamstime.com: James Byard tr,
Songquan Deng cla, John Sternig crb,
iStockphoto.com: LevKPhoto b.

Pull Out Map Cover

iStockphoto.com: LevKPhoto b.

All other images © Dorling Kindersley.
For further information see: www.dkimages.com

Printed and bound in China

First Edition 2004

Published in Great Britain by
Dorling Kindersley Limited
DK, One Embassy Gardens, 8 Viaduct
Gardens, London SW11 7BW, UK

The authorised representative in the EEA is
Dorling Kindersley Verlag GmbH. Arnulfstr.
124, 80636 Munich, Germany

Published in the United States by
DK US, 1450 Broadway, Suite 801,
New York, NY 10018, USA

Copyright © 2004, 2022
Dorling Kindersley Limited

A Penguin Random House Company

21 22 23 24 10 9 8 7 6 5 4 3 2 1

Reprinted with revisions 2006, 2008, 2010, 2012, 2014, 2017, 2019, 2022

A CIP catalog record is available
from the British Library.

A catalog record for this book is available
from the Library of Congress.

ISSN 1479-344X
ISBN 978-0-2415-5928-4

*As a guide to abbreviations in visitor
information blocks: Adm = admission charge*

MIX
Paper from
responsible sources
FSC™ C018179

This book was made with Forest Stewardship Council ™ certified paper – one small step in DK's commitment to a sustainable future. For more information go to www.dk.com/our-green-pledge

Selected Street Index

Chicago's Grid System

Nearly all streets in Chicago run east–west or north–south. The zero point is at the intersection of Madison Street (running east–west) and State Street (running north–south). All streets are labelled in relation to this point: for example, the section of State Street north of Madison is known as North State Street. Numbering also begins at the zero point and odd numbers are on the east sides of north–south streets and the south sides of east–west streets.